CW00664756

To Karen +

You are the best of

all the Vims faithful!

Yours,

Pat McMillan

Chris E...

John D...

William McMillan

PREVIOUS PAGE: Her engines exposed for scrutiny, the Vickers Vimy replica was tested above England by pilots Lang Kidby and Peter McMillan in August 1994.

THIS PAGE: Engineer Dan Nelson dug into the rear cockpit looking for yet another tool to continue the endless process of maintaining and tuning the gigantic biplane.

Dedicated to the memory of Steve Fossett, a pilot, a partner, a friend.

More than a thousand people played a critical role in the success of the Vimy Expeditions, but without the skills
and efforts of the following people the Vimy would have remained just another daydream.

Sebastien Arsenault, Patrick Bailey, Walter Boyne, Matt Bresler, Brooklands volunteers, Annette Carter,
Lyman Casey, Chris Condy, Wayne Daley, Lord Charles Denman, Iain Douglas-Hamilton, Erik Durfey,
Guy Edwards, Mick Follari, Robert Gieve, Bill Graves, Gil Grosvenor, Shaikh Hamad bin Ibrahim Al Khalifa,
Patrick Healy, Jackie Ireland, Gary Isaacs, ISTAT Foundation, Peter Jackson, Pat Joyce, Gary Kent,
Deirdre Keough, Bev Kidby, Gar Lasater, Don Lopez, John McBride, Dave McDowell, Tessa (Barroll) McMillan,
Roger McMullin, HRH Prince Michael of Kent, Peter Miller, Andy Morrison, Dan Nelson, Mark Nichols,
Derek Parker, Bill Patterson, Roger Pike, Bob Poole, Mike Potter, Patty Rebholz, Mick Reynolds,
Raymond Salisbury-Jones, Bob Shaw, William E. Simon, Mary Smith, Ken Smythe, Ian Snell, Joe Stancampiano,
Jim Stanfield, Jay Strauss, Gary Tierney, Christine Weber, Kevin Weldon, Bill Whitney, Malcolm Wood

On July 30, 1994, after 17 months
and more than 30,000 man-hours
of labor, the Vimy replica lifted
into the air on her maiden voyage.

AUTHOR
PETER MCMILLAN

PRINCIPAL PHOTOGRAPHERS
JAMES L. STANFIELD
PETER MCBRIDE

CONTRIBUTORS
PETER MCBRIDE
MARK REBHOLZ
JOHN LANOUE
PHILIP JARRETT

On July 3, 2005, a silver biplane prepared to joyfully meet the grass of Ireland after battling her way across the Atlantic Ocean in 18 hours and 19 minutes.

{ THE VIMY EXPEDITIONS }

VIMY

The Flying Machine that Moved Humanity

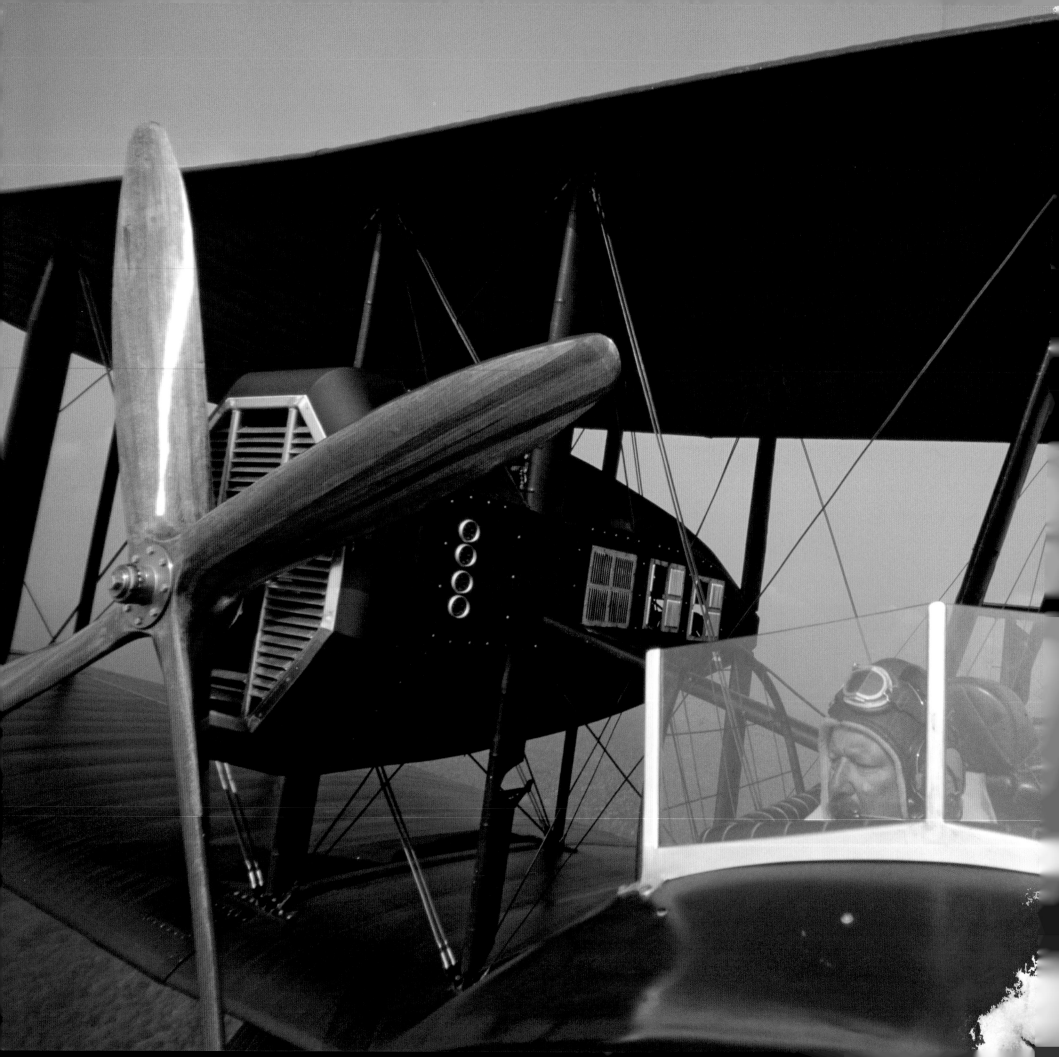

MAYDAY! MAYDAY! MAYDAY!

It was like a dream. No, a nightmare. We strained to see through the pungent smoke beneath us. The burning jungle seemed surreal, like an inferno. Our fate—or perhaps our epitaph—was down there, 1,800 feet below. The waiting would soon be over. We were fluttering down like an enormous kite with a broken string. The Vimy's right engine had shattered over the remote and inhospitable island of Sumatra.

"Mayday, Mayday, Mayday. Vimy One, Vimy One, Vimy One. We've had an engine failure," Lang Kidby called out to anyone on our radio frequency. "We're making an emergency landing." No response.

"See any place to land?" I yelled, as I struggled to maintain control against the asymmetric torque of the good engine.

"There's a small airfield 25 miles away," he said, scanning the chart.

"We'll never make it!" The muscles of my left leg were trembling as I held the rudder against our overwhelming momentum to the right. Even with the left engine operating, we were descending at 200 feet per minute.

Lang turned in the cramped confines of our cockpit. "What about that road on your side?" he asked, pointing to a dirt lane cut through the smoldering paddy fields.

I fought with both hands to bring her nose around to the left. Slightly obscured by the smoke, the road seemed narrow and was directly across the wind. But there weren't many other choices—only the dirt path, the burning jungle, or the rice paddies crisscrossed with retaining walls 20 yards apart.

Jim Stanfield, our veteran photographer from *National Geographic,* popped up from his seat in the nose. He snapped off a few shots of our motionless right prop, but he was blocking my view. "Jim, not now!" I yelled. "We're about to crash!" He dropped back into his seat.

As we descended to about 200 feet above the ground, I could see well enough to know that we were headed for disaster. The road was half the width we needed, and in the middle was a blue dump truck full of soil. As we bore down, several boys on bicycles dove headfirst into the deep ditches along the road.

"We can't use the road!" I shouted while shoving the throttle to the limit on the left engine. The burst of power pitched the nose up and swung the machine sharply to the right. I pulled hard to bring the wings level to stop us from cartwheeling. We braced for impact.
—Peter McMillan

After arriving in Australia, the crew flew along the east coast south of Coffs Harbour.

The *Silver Queen* clawed her way up to get a good view of Mt. Kenya on July 19, 1999, ultimately achieving an altitude of nearly 13,000 feet.

CONTENTS

The monuments at Giza to three pharaohs, Khufu, Khafre, and Menkaure, cast beautifully geometric shadows in the early morning light. On the flight to Australia in 1994 and again on the flight to South Africa in 1999, the crew was granted permission to photograph the pyramids.

The Vimy rested at Luskintyre farm, New South Wales, after her arduous first adventure covering more than 14,000 miles from London to and throughout Australia. She would remain in a hangar at Luskintyre for almost a year until the funds could be raised to resume her flying career.

The Vimy departed Pisa for Rome, but the flight was aborted due to strong headwinds, which reduced the ground speed to less than 10 miles per hour.

INTRODUCTION

by Peter McMillan What makes headlines in aviation today? Delays, crowded terminals, cramped seats, bad food—or no food. Occasionally one gets a glimpse of glory when a new airliner is launched that promises to take us farther, faster, higher, and with more comforts and greater luxury. Rarely today comes news of a crash, and when crashes do occur, they almost always have more to do with human error than any failing of technology.

It's hard to believe that just a few generations ago, at the close of World War I, most people thought of aviation as a folly, a stunt intrinsically dangerous and reckless. How aviation progressed was the work of a few men who forever changed the way we move around the world. They were brave, agile, and daring. No mere thrill seekers, they were supremely competent and excelled at the measurement of risk. These optimists bet that they could calculate the odds and win. They risked and they prevailed, proving timid skeptics wrong and inspiring those who came after them.

How did we first begin to move about the earth by air? Naturally, there was a bit of commercial opportunism involved.

The Great Air Races

In 1919, just after World War I, proponents of aviation and a few self-interested promoters arranged the first long-distance air races. London's *Daily Mail* and its inimitable owner, Lord Northcliffe, offered an enormous purse of £10,000 (more than $1 million today) to the first airmen who could cross the Atlantic.

The Australian government offered an identical purse to the winner of an 11,000-mile race across the British Empire from London to Australia. Finally, several British newspapers organized a race—and sponsored teams—to fly the length of the African continent. The first pilots to cover the almost 9,000 miles from London to Cape Town would win £10,000.

With few airports then in existence, and with weather forecasting still in its infancy, airmen in open cockpits endured the most horrendous physical conditions, not just in the air but on the ground—searing heat, frostbite, sandstorms, leeches, and attacks by marauding tribesmen. Contestants improvised engine repairs with chewing gum, and one team extracted its airplane from a muddy Asian field by lacing together a 1,200-foot bamboo runway made from the walls of local villagers' huts.

Despite the performance limitations of early airplanes, within a year all three events had been won. Englishmen John Alcock and Arthur Whitten Brown successfully crossed the Atlantic in just under 17 hours over the night of June 14–15, 1919, plowing gently into an Irish bog to claim the *Daily Mail* prize. Four other teams had failed; two were miraculously fished out of the frigid North Atlantic.

On December 10, 1919, Australian brothers Ross and Keith Smith and their resourceful mechanics, Jim Bennett and Wally Shiers, completed the Great Trans-Planet Air Race, flying from London to Australia in 28 days. Only one of the six other teams ever reached Australia, taking seven months to arrive. Finally, on March 20, 1920, South Africans Pierre van Ryneveld and C. J. Quintin Brand were the sole contestants to complete the London to Cape Town race. Because of numerous crashes and repairs, their flight took 43 days. (They were ineligible for the full prize due to changing aircraft as a result of the crashes.)

By spring of 1920, airplanes had linked the ends of the earth. Photographs taken by their pilots had given the world its first view from above such stunning landmarks and landscapes as the Taj Mahal and Victoria Falls. King George V bestowed knighthoods on the victors. Obituaries, however, came in greater numbers, leading to high controversy about these "races." Despite the tragedies, the world gained inspiration from the dash, the character, and the unquenchable optimism of the pilots who prevailed.

The names of these brave aeronauts belong next to those of Magellan, Columbus, and Captain James Cook; they were the first to explore the vastness of the sky. What did the crews who succeeded in these pioneering flights have in common? Winston Churchill summed it up as he presented the Atlantic prize to Alcock and Brown at a gala Savoy luncheon: "I don't know what we should admire most in our guests—their audacity, their determination, their skill, or their good fortune!"

The Other Common Denominator

These pilots had something else in common: they flew the same type of aircraft, the mammoth twin-engine Vickers F.B. (Fighting Biplane) 27, known as the Vimy.

Designed in 1918 as a night bomber and built by the Vickers factory at Brooklands, England, she arrived too late to see combat during the Great War. Powered by 360-horsepower, 20.5-liter Rolls-Royce Eagle VIII engines, she reigned in the postwar world as the "galleon of the skies."

Sadly, the sturdy majesty of the Vimy biplane was eclipsed in time by sleeker, faster designs. Vimys were used in the 1920s as parachute trainers, then were employed for crude blind-landing experiments in which the pilot trimmed the aircraft for landing at a height of 50 feet and let go of all controls. Some tattered Vimys that were still airworthy were relegated to a daily mail run from Cairo to Baghdad. By the 1930s, the records set by the Vimy had fallen.

Then, 73 years after the Smith brothers' epic flight from England to Australia, two friends had a dream.

The Dream

In 1992 my friend Lang Kidby and I were camping on Moreton Island, off the east coast of Australia. We had shared flying adventures in the past and were now considering fresh ones. Discussing aviation history, we noted that the record-setting Vickers Vimy had largely been forgotten, as had her contribution to drawing the world closer together.

A school group in Cape Town came to inspect the Vimy *Silver Queen* after her arrival from London—a feat that the original *Silver Queen* fell short of by 990 miles.

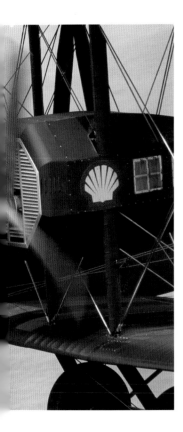

What an amazing experience it would be to re-create that galleon and to retrace early aviators' trails in the sky. To see the Taj Mahal again from a giant box kite at 70 miles per hour! We sensed that the reincarnation of this massive flying machine might remind the world that progress is achieved not by skeptics but by can-do risk takers like those who first flew the Vimy. We knew that if she could be rebuilt, this bundle of wood and wires could rekindle the spirit of adventure—that burning desire to discover what is over the horizon.

This simple idea led us to many adventures over the next 12 years, across 35 countries and nearly 30,000 miles. Thousands of good people helped us along the way, and often the efforts of a single individual on a given day advanced or saved the entire project. One was John LaNoue, the artist and craftsman who brought the Vimy to life, kept her running, and turned every bolt, knowing lives depended on it.

We are fortunate that our expeditions have been well recorded, thanks to the courage of Mary Smith, Peter Miller, and editor Bill Graves of *National Geographic.* Our 1994 voyage from London to Australia was the May 1995 cover story, documented through the lens of Jim Stanfield, one of the National Geographic Society's most prolific (and durable) photographers. A parallel film documentary, *The Greatest Flight,* was produced for NGTV by Christine Weber. The May 2000 *National Geographic* used the words and pictures of Peter McBride to illustrate our 1999 flight to Cape Town. Millions experienced the Vimy's dramatic 2005 crossing of the Atlantic, piloted by Mark Rebholz and the late Steve Fossett, on NationalGeographic.com.

Over these years, our team had to overcome tremendous obstacles, man-made as well as natural. We tried to succeed by emulating the attitudes of the pioneers, who relied on careful preparation, calculated risk taking, and professionalism on the ground and in the air. More often than not, we were lucky.

None of us involved at the inception of the Vimy project was blessed with independent wealth, so we were fortunate to have had the support of sponsors, including *National Geographic,* Shell, the Australian Army, the US Air Force, the Bahrain Committee, Federal Express, Rolls-Royce, Bose, and many others who championed the Vimy. Our flights never would have been possible without the financial generosity and logistical support of many individuals and families. Even in today's risk-averse world, they came forward to help us build wings to lift our dreams.

Here's to the risk takers! We invite you to explore the world with us, past and present.

FAR LEFT: The mammoth skeleton of the Vimy replica came together in the spring of 1994 at Hamilton Field, California. Approximately 30,000 man-hours of labor, led by John LaNoue, were required to construct the aircraft.

ABOVE: The forward crew positions are visible as the Vimy was flown above Sydney, Australia. The nose seat is the most comfortable, as it is well ahead of the propellers and the roar of the exhaust. The pilots experience earsplitting noise and the resonance from the prop tips—just nine inches from their ears.

LEFT: Lang Kidby inspected a crack in the left propeller shortly before the Vimy's departure from England to Australia.

BOTTOM LEFT: Wayne Daley, Lang Kidby, Peter McMillan, John LaNoue, and Dan Nelson (from left) gather in front of the emerging Vimy replica.

Cockpits Then and Now

The cockpit layout for the original Vickers F.B.27 Vimy (top) was generally duplicated in the modern incarnation (above). Designer Bill Whitney made a few enhancements for long-distance flying that were suggested by Peter McMillan and Lang Kidby at the outset of the Vimy project in 1992. In particular, the control wheel was movable so that the aircraft could be commanded from the right seat or left seat. The original Vimys had a fixed helm on the right side.

The Vimy replica also had to be fitted with a redundant electrical system, designed by Erik Durfey, to accommodate fuel injection and radios that would be critical to operate when the Vimy was in close proximity to sensitive national boundaries around warring regions in the Middle East, Africa, and Asia.

Although the cramped confines of the new cockpit were largely the same as those in the original aircraft, they offered the pilots a glorious perspective as the world unrolled before them, low and slow.

Most flying days started before dawn, with flight planning, military and civil clearances, weather forecasts, and inspections of the aircraft. It was usually a good day if the Vimy could depart with dew still on her broad wings.

The Vimy flew over eastern
Queensland on her victory lap
of Australia in October 1994.

{ 1919 | 1994 }

England to Australia

"God 'Elp All Of Us"

A few of the Notable British Records
in Human Achievement

apart from the Discoveries of JENNER (Vaccination); SIMPSON (Chloroform); HARVEY (Circulation of the Blood); MURDOCK (Coal Gas); YOUNG (Distillation of Paraffin Oil); BELL (Steam Navigation); COOK & WHEATSTONE (Electric Telegraph); NEWTON, DARWIN, ROSS, LISTER, PERKINS, etc.

FIRST STEAM ENGINE,
Watt—British.
FIRST DYNAMO,
Faraday—British.
FIRST DIRECT ATLANTIC FLIGHT, 1,890 Miles.
Royce Engines—British.

FIRST LOCOMOTIVE,
Stephenson—British.
FIRST STEAM TURBINE,
Parsons—British.
FIRST FLIGHT ENGLAND to AUSTRALIA, 11,294 miles.
Royce Engines—British.

THE FIRST

FLIGHT TO AUSTRALIA
was made with

ROLLS - ROYCE
AERO ENGINES

In a Vickers-Vimy-Rolls-Royce Aeroplane
piloted by Capt. ROSS SMITH, M.C., D.F.C., A.F.C.

THE FIRST DIRECT
FLIGHT ACROSS THE ATLANTIC
was also made with

ROLLS - ROYCE
AERO ENGINES,

In a Vickers-Vimy-Rolls-Royce Aeroplane
piloted by Capt. Sir JOHN ALCOCK, K.B.E., D.F.C.

ROLLS-ROYCE, LIMITED,
15-16, Conduit Street, London, W.1.
Telegrams—ROLHEAD, REG. LONDON.   Telephone—GERRARD 1654 (5 Lines)

Halfway Around the World

You have shown the world what manner of man the Australian is.
—A congratulatory telegram from Prime Minister Billy Hughes
to Captain Ross Smith

by Peter McMillan The press called it the Great Trans-Planet Air Race. The prize was £10,000—equivalent to more than a million dollars today. It was beyond the imagination, flying an airplane more than 11,000 miles in less than 30 days across the British Empire from England to Australia. "They are throwing dice with Death," complained the *London Times.* In fact, they were. Primitive engines; poor maps; few landing fields; formidable mountains, jungles, and oceans; disease; hostile tribesmen—all of these took a toll on the six teams that competed in the race. Only two crews ever arrived. The winners, an Australian crew led by Captain Ross Smith, took 28 days. The second-place team needed seven months. Cries from bereaved families of airmen lost in the race nearly brought down the Australian government for "sponsoring gladiators."

There was something special about Ross Smith. He was brave, nearly fearless. He was wounded at least five times as a soldier in the Middle East before he became an airman. His letters tell of the invigorating thrill of being under machine-gun fire. Though a country boy from a sheep farm, he was a born leader, able to calculate risks to a fine margin, and quickly. He knew his crew well: Keith, his older brother, served as navigator, just as he had in the Royal Flying Corps. Sergeants Jim Bennett and Wally Shiers, indispensable and creative mechanics who had served with Ross in the desert, were well acquainted with harsh conditions and scarce resources.

Their Vickers F.B.27 Vimy was the 10th of 330 Vimys, most of them built at Brooklands. She was given the registration G-EAOU. Ross, only half joking, said the letters stood for "God 'Elp All Of Us."

It seems that Ross Smith joined in the race truly for adventure, not for the glory. But imagine the adulation he would receive from his countrymen. He left Australia in 1914 a sheep farmer and a private soldier. When next

FAR LEFT: G-EAOU looked clean and shiny on the infield at Brooklands in England before her departure to Australia. It was here that Ross Smith quipped the registration actually meant "God 'Elp All Of Us."

TOP LEFT: Ross MacPherson Smith in Australian Flying Corps uniform (left) and Keith MacPherson Smith in Royal Flying Corps uniform (right). Ross, who also served as an enlisted soldier, was awarded a battlefield commission in the Middle East campaign of World War I.

TOP: On December 11, 1919, the day after the arrival of G-EAOU, Rolls-Royce placed an advertisement in the *London Times* trumpeting the flight to Australia as well as the Atlantic crossing in the Vimy flown by John Alcock and Arthur Whitten Brown.

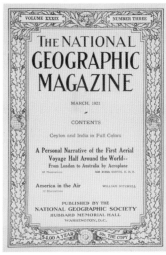

ABOVE: In one of the longest articles to appear in *National Geographic,* Ross Smith published his account of the flight. He described with great flair the sights, smells, and textures of the earth to the rapt readers, but reported mishaps and near death experiences with characteristic understatement.

he saw his mother, five years later, he was a knight commander of the British Empire, and a friend of generals and T. E. Lawrence. Australia had arrived. Its people rejoiced.

Hounslow Heath, England—November 12, 1919, 9:10 a.m.

Ross and his intrepid fellow Aussies departed from a scrubby field that is now the southern boundary of Heathrow Airport. The heath was dusted with snow; the local weather was declared Class 5, which contemporary manuals translate as "totally unfit for flying." Exposed to the elements in the open cockpit, Ross noted in his log: "This sort of flying is a rotten game. The cold is hell. I am a silly ass for ever having embarked on this flight." The crew's sandwiches froze en route. Ross, though, had little time to waste complaining. Other competitors had already departed, and the prize meant security for life. Amazingly, Keith managed to dead reckon them by compass to Lyon, France, in just under six hours, hardly ever sighting ground.

Misadventures followed. The winter mud of Italy nearly stuck the Vimy to the ground until spring. Had it not been for Bennett pushing on the tail (and being pulled aboard by Shiers), and for Ross's superb technique— accelerating between the pond-sized puddles—they never would have lifted off from Pisa. Ross declared that the takeoff through the whirling mud "must have resembled that of a seaplane."

The crew crossed the Mediterranean from Suda Bay in Crete to Egypt, first with little—and then with no—survival gear. Shiers and Bennett began the flight sitting in their aft cockpit atop four partially inflated inner tubes. As the Vimy gained altitude, the tubes inflated, pushing the mechanics up and nearly out of their tiny hole. Shiers punctured one of the tubes with his jackknife, then paused, looked at Bennett, and punctured the other three. They were all in this adventure together now.

The sight of the Nile Delta and Alexandria buoyed them. On landing, they were happy to lounge in the wicker chairs on the veranda of Cairo's Shepheard's Hotel and enjoy a cool drink. The scene was familiar to Ross from his visits during the war. The Vimy was tied down at the Royal Air Force aerodrome in Heliopolis, near Cairo, which gave Bennett and Shiers a chance to complete much-needed maintenance and repairs. Among other problems, G-EAOU's right engine had been overheating. Shiers passed out Wrigley's gum to the puzzled crew, then retrieved the wads and combined them into a mass big enough to spread over a crack in one of the cooling water pipes. He wrapped the pipe and the gum with electrical tape, finally coating the repair with shellac. They took a test flight around the pyramids. All was well for them to push east.

The Vimy left Cairo for Damascus on November 18. Sandstorms and even sleet plagued them in the air and on the ground as they crossed Iraq in two legs, forced to land to make repairs to control surfaces and cables damaged in extreme turbulence. The crew spent the night of November 20 holding on to the machine as a wet desert wind blew in with force. Conditions were harsh, but their suffering was tempered by the news that as many as four other contestants had died in the race. A few days of fair weather enabled the Vimy to make it all the way to Delhi by November 25 —she had traveled 1,600 miles in 25 flying hours and only 54 hours of

TOP: On the snowy day of departure, November 12, 1919, a small crowd including officials from the Royal Aero Club bade the Australians bon voyage. The tall man just below the left propeller hub (between mechanics Wally Shiers and Jim Bennett) is Rex Pierson, designer of the Vickers F.B.27 Vimy.

ABOVE: In below-freezing temperatures across the Alps, Ross noted the unpleasant conditions in his diary, declaring himself to be "a silly ass for ever having embarked on this flight."

TOP LEFT: G-EAOU underwent routine maintenance on the horse-racing track in Singapore. As with many of her arrivals, she was the first aircraft to land there, so improvisation was required by the resourceful crew. The race course was so small that the Vimy's wheels took a number of tree branches upon takeoff.

LEFT: The Vimy headed eastward across Indonesia.

TOP: In Surabaya, local people used bamboo mats to extract the Vimy from the mud after she broke through the thin, dry crust on the field.

ABOVE: The villagers made a makeshift runway of bamboo and reed mats from their huts. The Vimy finally departed from a predicament that at first seemed as if it would cost the team their prize after flying nearly halfway around the world.

LEFT: Mechanics Wally Shiers (left) and Jim Bennett made ingenious repairs with ordinary materials. They filled a fissure in an intake pipe with chewing gum and fixed a cracked propeller with splinters from a fruit crate and brass screws from the instrument panel.

TOP LEFT: On the island of Timor, three of the Australian crew, Shiers, Bennett, and Ross Smith (from left), raised their coconuts and drank to their success as they prepared for the final leg to Australia.

TOP RIGHT: On their victory lap across Australia, the crew took tea at an outback settlement.

ABOVE: Keith Smith hoisted the Rolls-Royce Eagle VIII engine into place after extensive repairs when the engine failed near Charleville, Queensland, on December 25, 1919. Sensitive to public relations, Ross said the engine had not failed but merely "quit in protest at being put to work on Christmas Day."

elapsed time. They soared above the Taj Mahal, which Ross described as "a matchless white jewel reclining in a setting of Nature's emeralds." On the way to Calcutta, a raptor flew into the starboard propeller with a great crash of wood and feathers. Amazingly, the prop held together, but they would remain suspicious of it, as the right side would begin knocking in the coming weeks.

On December 2, the Vimy crew narrowly averted disaster. Despite the lack of airfields in Southeast Asia, they had been informed that one had been cleared for them near Singora, Siam (now Thailand). Upon arrival, they circled overhead in disbelief. The trees had been cut, but none of the stumps had been removed. There were no other options save the ocean or the jungle, so Ross slowed the Vimy as much as possible before touchdown and miraculously missed most of the largest stumps, though the tail skid broke away after contacting a smaller one.

Ross and Keith enhanced the "aerodrome" at Singora and after two days made their escape, alighting on the small race course in Singapore, much to the surprise of the horse fans, few of whom had ever seen an airplane. Taking off from so small a pitch with obstacles all around was breathtaking for Ross. The Vimy took a few tree branches with her.

Ross turned the aircraft left toward Batavia (now Jakarta) in Java, stopping at the local Dutch headquarters at Kalijati. There were but six days to run, and tensions were rising. A stop at Surabaya was to be routine, but under the dusty surface where they landed, the crust broke through to reveal an underlayer of mud. It took the crew more than an hour to dig out the wheels and move the ship a few feet, where she quickly sank again. She was hopelessly bogged. For the Smith brothers, the race was over, less than a thousand miles from home—or so it seemed.

A few villagers brought bamboo mats, which were used to support the weight of the mammoth flying machine once she was wrestled out again. An idea took hold. Soon villagers streamed into the open field, carrying mats from their dismantled huts. Within a few hours, a two-lane runway of about 1,200 feet was fashioned from the mats. The first attempted takeoff was a failure, as the prop wash blew the mats in all directions and the Vimy slewed clumsily into the mud. The team then pegged the mats, and the Vimy, airborne, made course for Australia, heading for the home stretch.

The Vimy made two more long legs down the chain of islands, and at dawn, on December 10, 1919, the four Australians left the Dutch East Indies (present-day Indonesia) bound for Darwin. The crossing was routine, though they flew entirely over shark-infested waters. They touched "Terra Australis" at 2:50 p.m. They had won, and they had survived.

The race was over, but the team elected to fly home to Adelaide—a decision that brought with it another series of near death adventures. The right propeller disintegrated in western Queensland, about halfway home. For almost two months, they were stuck making repairs near the outback town of Charleville, a venue that would come to have some significance for us more than seven decades later.

At last they made it home—first to Sydney, then to Melbourne, then finally to Adelaide. Ross hugged his mother for the first time in five long years. Her boy, the farmhand, now Captain Sir Ross Smith, had come home.

LEFT: The Vimy arrived triumphant at Mascot Aerodrome in Sydney on February 14, 1920. Thousands came to see the first aircraft to fly all the way from England.

BELOW: Ross Smith reunited with his mother, Jessie, after five years. Upon leaving the family sheep station in 1914, he had become a private soldier, been wounded five times, and learned to fly. He returned by air as a knight commander of the British Empire.

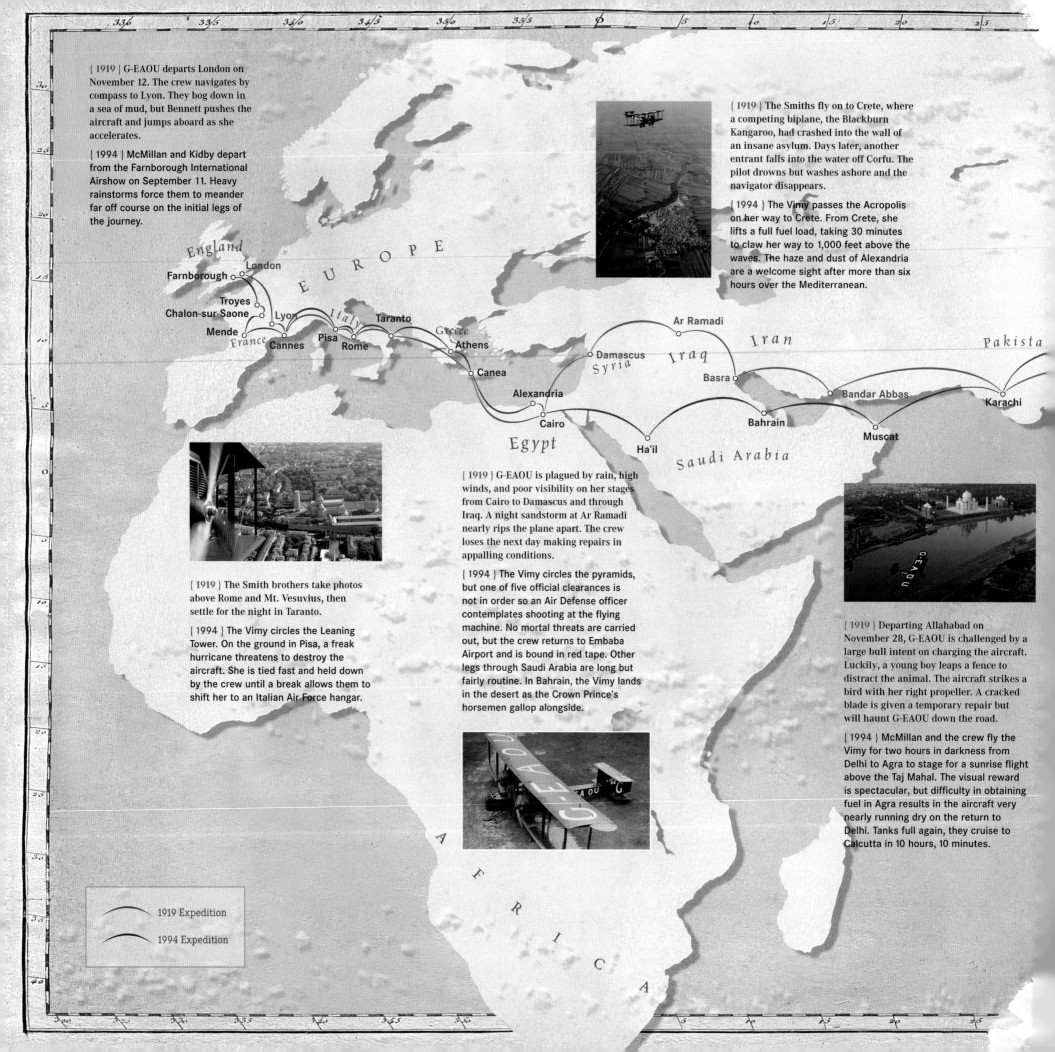

{ 1919 } G-EAOU departs London on November 12. The crew navigates by compass to Lyon. They bog down in a sea of mud, but Bennett pushes the aircraft and jumps aboard as she accelerates.

{ 1994 } McMillan and Kidby depart from the Farnborough International Airshow on September 11. Heavy rainstorms force them to meander far off course on the initial legs of the journey.

{ 1919 } The Smiths fly on to Crete, where a competing biplane, the Blackburn Kangaroo, had crashed into the wall of an insane asylum. Days later, another entrant falls into the water off Corfu. The pilot drowns but washes ashore and the navigator disappears.

{ 1994 } The Vimy passes the Acropolis on her way to Crete. From Crete, she lifts a full fuel load, taking 30 minutes to claw her way to 1,000 feet above the waves. The haze and dust of Alexandria are a welcome sight after more than six hours over the Mediterranean.

{ 1919 } The Smith brothers take photos above Rome and Mt. Vesuvius, then settle for the night in Taranto.

{ 1994 } The Vimy circles the Leaning Tower. On the ground in Pisa, a freak hurricane threatens to destroy the aircraft. She is tied fast and held down by the crew until a break allows them to shift her to an Italian Air Force hangar.

{ 1919 } G-EAOU is plagued by rain, high winds, and poor visibility on her stages from Cairo to Damascus and through Iraq. A night sandstorm at Ar Ramadi nearly rips the plane apart. The crew loses the next day making repairs in appalling conditions.

{ 1994 } The Vimy circles the pyramids, but one of five official clearances is not in order so an Air Defense officer contemplates shooting at the flying machine. No mortal threats are carried out, but the crew returns to Embaba Airport and is bound in red tape. Other legs through Saudi Arabia are long but fairly routine. In Bahrain, the Vimy lands in the desert as the Crown Prince's horsemen gallop alongside.

{ 1919 } Departing Allahabad on November 28, G-EAOU is challenged by a large bull intent on charging the aircraft. Luckily, a young boy leaps a fence to distract the animal. The aircraft strikes a bird with her right propeller. A cracked blade is given a temporary repair but will haunt G-EAOU down the road.

{ 1994 } McMillan and the crew fly the Vimy for two hours in darkness from Delhi to Agra to stage for a sunrise flight above the Taj Mahal. The visual reward is spectacular, but difficulty in obtaining fuel in Agra results in the aircraft very nearly running dry on the return to Delhi. Tanks full again, they cruise to Calcutta in 10 hours, 10 minutes.

England
London
Farnborough
Troyes
Chalon-sur-Saone
Mende
Lyon
Cannes
Pisa
Rome
Taranto
Athens
Canea
Alexandria
Cairo
Damascus
Ar Ramadi
Basra
Bahrain
Ha'il
Bandar Abbas
Muscat
Karachi

EUROPE
France
Italy
Greece
Syria
Iraq
Iran
Pakista
Egypt
Saudi Arabia
AFRICA

1919 Expedition
1994 Expedition

{ 1919 } G-EAOU, flying beyond the territory that has ever seen an aircraft, lands at horse-racing tracks on several occasions and a purpose-built landing ground in Thailand where the stumps were never cleared from the area. The crew pushes on, becoming the first aircraft to cross the equator on December 6.

{ 1994 } The crew has difficulty entering Myanmar, as they were in India during an outbreak of plague, which results in a temporary halt of all incoming flights. More problematic is the right engine. It begins to oscillate slightly but uncontrollably.

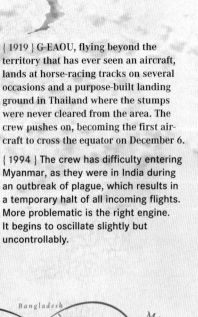

God 'Elp All Of Us

ENGLAND TO AUSTRALIA
1919 | 1994

{ 1919 } The Smith brothers, Bennett, and Shiers land in Surabaya, but the aircraft breaks through the dry, crusty surface into a mire of mud. Local villagers bring mats to support the aircraft, which sparks an idea. Hundreds of locals dismantle their huts and use the bamboo matting to build a runway. G-EAOU makes a miraculous escape.

{ 1994 } When the Vimy experiences engine failure on October 9, McMillan urgently maneuvers the wounded bird to a forced landing in a dry paddy. No one is injured, but the earthen dividing walls of the paddy smash the undercarriage. Kidby leads a team of local farmers to knock down the walls and carve out a landing strip. The Vimy flies to Jakarta six days later with temporary repairs.

{ 1919 } At Ward Plain, near Charleville, Queensland, Australia, G-EAOU suffers a complete engine failure. She is forced to land on December 25, in part due to the vibrations of the propeller that was cracked by a bird strike in India. The crew makes repairs for seven weeks, then refuels and heads on to Sydney, Melbourne, and Adelaide.

{ 1994 } On October 28, McMillan, Kidby, Nelson, and Stanfield land in Charleville and explore the scrubland around Ward Plain. They find battered and rusty fuel cans that were discarded 75 years earlier by Ross Smith and his crew.

{ 1919 } Ross Smith lands the first aircraft ever to fly to Australia on December 10. He and Keith are greeted as international heroes and are later knighted by King George V. They completed the voyage in 28 days, just under the deadline to win the £10,000 prize. Ross divides the prize equally among the four airmen.

{ 1994 } McMillan and Kidby land on October 22. Their voyage took 42 days due to red tape, quarantine, and the crash in Sumatra, but the well-worn flying machine has come halfway around the world.

ASIA

Bangladesh

Calcutta

Myanmar

Thailand

Yangon

Bangkok

Songkhla

Langkawi
Penang
Sitiawan

Malaysia

Singapore

Sumatra

Palembang

Kalijati

Atambua

Crash Site

Jakarta

Java

Surabaya

Bali

Sumbawa

Bima

Timor

Kupang

Darwin

Warlock Ponds

Newcastle Waters

Tennant Creek

Cloncurry

Longreach

Charleville

Oakey

Brisbane

Bourke

Coffs Harbour

Cootamundra
Henty

Sydney

Australia

Adelaide

Melbourne

Mittagong

LEFT: A crowd lined up to witness the Vimy's departure from the Farnborough International Airshow. Engines turning, the Vimy waited for a ceremonial flypast of a Qantas 747 to wish the crew well for their long reach to Australia.

ABOVE: Pilots for the journey to Australia were Peter McMillan (top), an American investment banker who left his career to pursue the dream of flying the Vimy, and Lang Kidby, a serial adventurer and retired Australian Army pilot.

"God 'Elp All Of Us"...Again

by Peter McMillan We came to England in August 1994, throwing ourselves into a two-week flurry of activity—press conferences, test flying, prop balancing, riveting, flight planning—all 20-odd crew members moving apart, then coming back together every few days at Brooklands Museum in Surrey. Rolls-Royce hosted a ceremonial send-off luncheon for us at Farnborough, but Lang Kidby and I were obliged to make ready before the first bites were served. Jim Stanfield, perhaps the most prolific of *National Geographic*'s photographers, mounted the seat in the Vimy's bow, while Dan Nelson, our tireless engineer, took a seat in the aft cockpit.

On takeoff at 2:05 p.m. on September 11, we were escorted by a Qantas 747 flying alongside Runway 24 at Farnborough. Mesmerized for a moment, Lang encouraged me to turn a bit more to the left to give wide berth to the jumbo's vortices. We continued our left turn toward France, and the adventure was under way.

We started across the English Channel near Firle Beacon, Sussex. Rain came, and clouds darkened. The excitement and the glamour quickly gave way to traces of doubt and even fear. At such times, focusing the mind on practical problems helps restore one's emotions to an even keel. In this case, our compass, which had been behaving erratically, came off its mount and fell into Lang's lap. That gave us something to focus on.

Compass fixed, we made our way to the town of Troyes, in the Champagne region of France, where we were greeted with two magnums of Pol Roger hand-delivered by the owner. The following stages were indirect at best, as we managed around storms, mountains, and sponsor appearances. Lang and I were still learning to handle the Vimy. We had less than 40 hours flying time and were just beginning to try her with very heavy loads and with turbulence, hard rain, icy clouds, restricted airspace, and pilot fatigue.

Near Disaster in Italy

A freak hurricane in Pisa, Italy, nearly rolled the Vimy into a ball of canvas and matchsticks on September 15. The storm's first wave deposited four inches of rain in a half hour. Winds reached 70 miles per hour. Ten of us, assisted by multiple ropes, strained to hold her fast. An Italian Air Force general, Domenico Mazza, offered us one of his huge hangars across the airport, so we dashed about during the eye of the storm and taxied the Vimy to shelter, closing the doors as the gale returned and the winds reached 80 miles per hour. Late that afternoon, we surveyed the devastation around the city: trees had been downed, and cranes snapped. Even the famous Leaning Tower seemed to be listing a bit more.

DEPARTURE: September 11, 1994; Farnborough, England

ARRIVAL: October 22, 1994; Darwin, Australia

DURATION: 42 days and 11,234 miles

PILOTS: Peter McMillan and Lang Kidby

LOGISTICS AND SUPPORT: Tessa Barroll, Bev Kidby, Dan Nelson, Mark Rebholz, Mick Reynolds, Bob Shaw, Ian Snell, Gary Tierney

The flying days improved as we pushed south to Rome, across Mt. Vesuvius to Taranto, then to Athens and to Suda Bay in Crete. There was no land between us and Africa, only 540 miles of Mediterranean Sea. Lang and I donned life vests and for the first time, in the early hours of September 20, took to the air with a full fuel load of 4,500 pounds. The Vimy's initial climb performance was appalling; she took 30 minutes to reach 1,000 feet above the waves. Lang and I also had to closely monitor the gauges for overheating. We were in sweltering air, unable to climb where it was cooler, yet needing maximum power to keep the swollen beast aloft at all.

After six and a half hours, the winds were slightly behind us, and we were relieved to see Alexandria. I was particularly pleased when we squeaked on to the worn runway at Embaba Airport in Cairo, since success to this point enabled us to earn a substantial progress payment from our major sponsor. I immediately wired the funds to reduce the substantial overdraft in my account—all part of the adventure.

Our flight above the pyramids was glorious the following dawn, but was nearly brought to an abrupt end by a zealous Egyptian Air Defense officer who had not been briefed about our multilayered permissions to conduct the flight. We were tethered to the ground the next day by red tape and dense fog, then finally cut loose for Saudi Arabia.

In the Path of T. E. Lawrence…Almost

I was finally beginning to live out some of the precious daydreams of the past: drifting by the ancient monuments, over Suez, the Red Sea, the Hejaz railway, the vast An Nafud Desert; chasing wild camels; reliving the exploits of Captain Ross Smith, of T. E. Lawrence, of the Bedouins. I suddenly was jerked back to the present by the radio: "Vimy, how high are you? You are instructed to fly at 11,000 feet!" "Yes sir," I replied, "we are still climbing." Not only were we straining to reach our maximum height of 2,000 feet, but I didn't dare tell him that our map had blown out the cockpit, and we weren't exactly sure of our position.

Hospitality improved when we reached Ha'il and was overwhelming in Bahrain. The government hosted a series of events, including a festive landing in the desert, all organized by our dear friend Shaikh Hamad bin Ibrahim Al Khalifa. We said good-bye and headed down the Persian Gulf, touching down in Muscat before crossing the Gulf of Oman to Pakistan.

From Karachi, border conflicts made it nearly impossible for us to get into India. Then an outbreak of plague made it nearly impossible to get out, as all international flights were grounded. Mark Rebholz and Mick Reynolds did a masterful job navigating us around bureaucracies and quarantines. With 4,000-pound fuel loads and high tropical temperatures, the Vimy was grounded for the day if not airborne by sunrise, given that the flight legs were 10 to 12 hours. But with great difficulties came great rewards. The Taj Mahal glowed pink beneath our wings in the light of the Indian dawn, like a giant pearl, as Ross Smith described.

Once past the terrifying terrain of Myanmar, we celebrated on arrival in Bangkok, Thailand. After all, we had conquered hurricanes, plague, border wars, formidable mountains, vast amounts of water, and miles of red

The Vimy's nose position is fairly quiet since it is ahead of the propellers. It also offers a spectacular view. Normally, the pilot who is flying sits on the left, while the pilot who is not flying sits on the right and handles radio and navigation duties. The propellers are only about nine inches from their ears. The aft cockpit, not shown here, receives the full blast from the propellers and the engine noise.

After leaving the safety of England, the reborn G-EAOU pushed out over the English Channel. The flight was cold but went off without a hitch.

tape—in a primitive flying machine that had been airworthy for only eight weeks. The crew was jubilant. It would be all downhill to Australia, as long as the engines kept turning.

Flying on One Engine

Complaints from the right engine began as Lang and I were on an unpleasant four-hour scud run across the Malay Peninsula. We ducked around low clouds and high rocks, often obliged to skim the dense jungle below. The motor was oscillating slowly but uncontrollably. Lang yelled to me, "Mate, where's the nearest airfield?" Serious words, indeed. We landed at an overgrown, abandoned World War II airstrip, much to the delight of kids from the adjacent school. After tinkering, we pushed on to Singapore, having changed the spark plugs and everything else we could. She seemed to sound better—or maybe we tried to hear less. We passed the equator with Dan Nelson in the back and photographer Jim Stanfield in his usual seat in the nose. Over Sumatra, the clouds morphed into dense smoke from out-of-control slash and burn fires, forcing us to fly no more than 200 feet above the jungle. We dared not lose sight of the ground.

The right engine began acting up again. By turning into the wind and heading toward the coast of the Java Sea, I was able to climb to 1,800 feet while maintaining marginal visibility of the burning terrain below. Suddenly, without hearing a bang, I watched in disbelief as the tach needle wilted to zero. The Vimy was controllable on one engine, but even with my best technique she would return to earth in just a few minutes. The bit of extra height saved us. We were able to survey the options and choose a rice field rather than spear into the jungle, which would have been the outcome had we stayed on our original course. Jim was briefly a minor hazard: gripped by the moment, he stood in the nose taking pictures of the motionless right propeller. I "encouraged" him to strap in for the landing.

We swept into the smoldering field gently at first, then smashed into a matrix of low earthen walls, breaking the Vimy's axles and her tail wheel. At least we were all in one piece. The exception was the right engine. It was in many jagged pieces.

Seemingly out of nowhere, a large crowd of farmers gathered, many with lit cigarettes, and leaned against our highly flammable machine. A quick survey of the situation left me in despair. The project, the adventure, the life savings—it was all over. Lang saw the circumstances differently.

The Phoenix Rises

Within a few days, Lang had organized the farmers into constructing an airfield from the dry paddy. Very familiar with third-world operations, he knew the right mixture of encouragement, incentives, and cajoling to get the job done. He was inspiring. Our spare engine was flown to us quite bravely by Mick Reynolds in the twin-engine Nomad, lent to us by the Australian Army. Our team reunited, and on the sixth day, we flew off to Jakarta. After a few more days spent completing repairs, we were finally on our way to Australia.

The last legs—island hopping eastward—did not offer any second chances. Rugged volcanic terrain, long water crossings, constant headwinds, and

Plagued with foul weather across Europe, the Vimy crew arrived soaking wet at the end of each day and rarely at their intended destination. A few spectacular vistas like this rainbow over the Loire Valley made the diversions bearable.

persistent turbulence did not enhance my self-confidence. The voices of doubt became constant companions.

From Timor, Lang took the controls for the eight-and-a-half-hour sea crossing to his native Australia. I was naming the minutes, fumbling with the map, hearing strange noises from the engine…or not? Lang pushed on, just wanting badly to get home. As usual, his fortitude made the difference.

I saw Bathurst Island first, then the red soil of the mainland, then Darwin. As Lang pulled the throttles back for landing, the wires were singing. I took a deep breath.

Amid the celebration that followed, I looked back at the Vimy's broad wings. Inscriptions and greetings in many languages were traced into the dusty fabric. I recalled the words of Ross Smith: "The hardships and perils of the past month were forgotten in the excitement of the present. We shook hands with one another, our hearts swelling with those emotions invoked by achievement and the glamour of the moment. It was, and will be, perhaps, the supreme hour of our lives."

Nomad to the Rescue

The support plane that came to our aid after the Vimy crashed in Sumatra was a Nomad, a twin-engine turboprop. Supplied by the Australian Army Aviation Corps, the plane and its crew—pilot Major Mick Reynolds, copilot Gary Tierney, and engineer Bob Shaw—were critical to the success of the project. The Nomad had a limited range, and had to fly higher and faster than the Vimy for fuel economy, but was capable of landing on very rough airstrips. The Vimy was in contact with the Nomad by radio half the time. Once or twice a day, we saw the Nomad, which carried a *National Geographic* crew and its equipment, and served as a base for taking aerial photographs of the Vimy. The Nomad was in Jakarta when the Vimy lost one engine and had to land in Sumatra. Miraculously, by estimating the Vimy's flight path and despite the appalling visibility, Mick Reynolds was able to find the plane and crew. Three days after the crash landing, he expertly alighted, bringing a replacement engine, tools, food, and much-needed good cheer.

ABOVE: After hours of flying through heavy rain and dodging clouds and mountain peaks, the Vimy found the haven of an airstrip on a plateau near Mende, France. Foul weather had pushed the crew more than 100 miles off course, but they felt relieved to return safely to terra firma.

RIGHT TOP: The Vimy glided past Monte Carlo. The crew briefly considered stopping for a turn at the famous casino, but it was September 13 so they elected to push on to Pisa, Italy.

RIGHT: Crossing the Maritime Alps was wet and cold, and rarely involved flying in a straight line. Peter and Lang could see only a few miles ahead, which forced them to alter course each time they came upon a mountain ridge or wall of clouds.

FAR RIGHT: On the approach to Mende, the town's key landmark, a 14th-century cathedral, stood out. "When you have to fly low enough to navigate by cathedrals," Peter later remarked, "it's time to find a place to land."

Though a large aircraft, essentially the Boeing 747 of its day, the Vickers Vimy is primitive and vulnerable to the elements. Here she has clawed her way above the clouds of Europe, but more often her performance limitations left the crew unable to go over or around bad weather. It then became a matter of gripping the wheel with both hands and riding her through the storm.

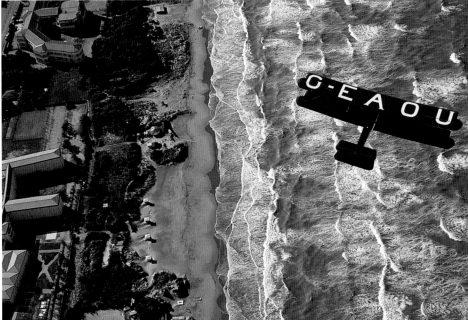

LEFT: Pisa and the Leaning Tower were shot from the nose of the Vimy by Joe Stancampiano, *National Geographic* photo engineer. After battling clouds from southern France, which pushed the Vimy into the Ligurian Sea, the crew broke into glorious sunlight approaching the medieval trading center.

TOP: Dan Nelson and the other crew members struggled to hold the aircraft down against the force of a freak hurricane in Pisa. Winds reached 80 miles per hour.

ABOVE: Lang Kidby (left) and Mark Rebholz took shelter during a lull in the hurricane but maintained a firm grasp on the aileron horns.

RIGHT TOP: Fighting a crosswind, the Vimy flew south along the beaches of Italy.

RIGHT BOTTOM: Fair skies returned as the Vimy passed fabled Mt. Vesuvius. The crew enjoyed a magical view of the Apennines.

LEFT: The Vimy's letters started to disappear into the blackness of a storm cloud as she neared Taranto, Italy. Once again, the Vimy was a rainmaker: the crew finished yet another day soaked to the bone.

ABOVE: Across the Mediterranean, the Vimy passed her toughest test yet. Temperatures were very hot, and the crew had to alternate climbing and gliding down at idle power to cool the engines. The coast of Egypt was a gladsome sight, as was the Nile Delta near Alexandria.

LEFT: In the bronze light of a desert dawn, the Vimy looked modern against the ancient pyramids at Giza. The big box kite seemed to be a reminder that a hundred years is just a split second in this region's long history. Of the seven wonders of the ancient world, only the pyramids remain.

TOP: Flying in the Middle East required hours of planning, as most areas are restricted. On several occasions, civilian aircraft wandering off course had been shot down. Peter studied a map before departure from Cairo to Saudi Arabia. His map later blew out of his hands in the windy cockpit. He and Lang then elected to fly below radar and dead reckoned their way to Ha'il.

ABOVE: The Vimy gathered speed on takeoff from Cairo's decrepit Embaba Airport. Her tanks were full for the 10-hour flight to Saudi Arabia, so she labored for more than an hour to reach 2,000 feet above the ground. The air controllers became exasperated when the crew could not comply with instructions to fly at 11,000 feet. Peter merely explained, "We're still climbing to assigned altitude!"

ABOVE: The Vimy flew over the rugged An Nafud Desert in northern Saudi Arabia.

RIGHT: During interviews, one of the questions was always, "You've just landed from flying 10 hours. Where did you go to the toilet?"

RIGHT BOTTOM: Peter (left) and Lang enjoyed an audience with the late Shaikh Isa bin Salman Al Khalifa, Emir of Bahrain. "I will never forget the delightful smell of cardamom coffee," Peter recalled.

FAR RIGHT: The Bahrain government hosted a spectacle in the desert with the Crown Prince's Ceremonial Guard galloping their fine Arabian horses alongside the Vimy as she landed.

LEFT: After a long flight across Saudi Arabia, the Vimy glided toward the lights of Bahrain. The crew was greeted on arrival by a trumpet fanfare, young girls bearing bouquets of flowers, and a bounty of local food.

ABOVE AND RIGHT: Admirers young and old enjoyed the music and traditional dancing, as well as the flying display. A special guest was the Crown Prince, Shaikh Hamad bin Isa Al Khalifa, who arrived flying his own helicopter. The three-day stop in Bahrain gave the crew a much-needed opportunity to perform maintenance and repairs on their flying machine. She had flown nearly 6,000 miles with limited attention through very harsh conditions.

LEFT: Much of infrastructure in India in the mid-1990s, such as the Calcutta airport shown here, was in a decrepit state.

BELOW LEFT: Red lines on the chart show the confused situation faced by the Vimy crew as they tried to cross the frontier between Pakistan and India. The Pakistanis approved a flight clearance to the north with a right turn to Delhi, while the Indians offered a clearance to the south with a left dogleg to Delhi. The northern clearance crossed high terrain beyond the capability of the fully loaded Vimy. The southern clearance would land them in an area quarantined due to an outbreak of plague. Eventually the warring governments relented and let the Vimy fly a fairly straight line up the middle.

BELOW: Three of the challenges of the long flights across the Indian subcontinent were, from top, finding fuel, extensive flight planning and replanning, and starting each day hours before dawn. The crew needed at least five different approval stamps on their flight plan, in triplicate, before each departure, including air defense clearance, customs, and air traffic control. An added concern was that the Vimy had to be airborne no later than sunrise or she could not climb in the Indian daytime heat.

ABOVE: Tracking down the Yamuna River just after dawn brought into view the Taj Mahal, its dome glowing pink like a giant pearl. Lingering over this magnificent sight came with a price. The Vimy did not have enough fuel to get back to Delhi and had to land at Agra Air Force Station, which had only jet fuel. The crew hitched a ride to town, found a leaky barrel, and filled it with "mystery juice" from a station servicing only scooters. The fuel did not agree with the Vimy's engines and would extract a greater price later on.

First Above the Taj Mahal

On November 27, 1919, Captain Ross Smith leaned over the side of the Vimy to take this photograph of the Taj Mahal, which is believed to be the first aerial shot of the world-famous landmark. The Taj was built in the 17th century by Mogul Emperor Shah Jahan as a mausoleum for his favorite wife, Mumtaz Mahal. "Of all the remembered scenes, wonderful and beautiful," Ross declared, "the Taj Mahal remains the most beautiful and the most exquisite."

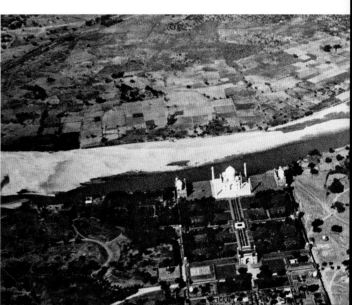

Positioning the Vimy for a sunrise flight over the Taj Mahal entailed logistical headaches and hazards, such as flying two hours in darkness the night before from Delhi to Agra. Despite these risks, orbiting the Taj was a stunning experience. Peter recalled, "It was just as Ross described, pink like a pearl, and I was amazed at the immense size and perfect symmetry of the structure." Upon returning to Agra, *National Geographic* photographer Jim Stanfield exclaimed, "I think we got the cover!" And he did—for the May 1995 issue of the magazine.

FAR LEFT: The Vimy threaded her way through Three Pagodas Pass, which marks the border between Myanmar and Thailand. The menacing terrain meant that any mechanical problem would have spelled disaster, which the pilots thought about hour after hour above the dense vegetation. At one point, looking down at the 80-foot-high canopy, Lang yelled to Peter, "Mate, they wouldn't find us for a hundred years!"

LEFT: The spire at the holy Buddhist temple of Shwedagon in Yangon contains a 76-karat diamond. A temple has been on this site for 2,500 years. The present structure dates to 1769, when the temple was largely rebuilt after an earthquake.

BELOW FAR LEFT AND LEFT CENTER: Photographer Jim Stanfield, a veteran of many missions to Myanmar, spent an afternoon capturing various street scenes.

BELOW: All commercial flights from India had been canceled due to a plague outbreak, so when the Vimy was denied permission to enter Myanmar, the crew turned off their radio. Upon approaching Yangon, the pilots were given permission to land. Once on the ground, they were immediately examined by doctors for plague symptoms and were quickly released.

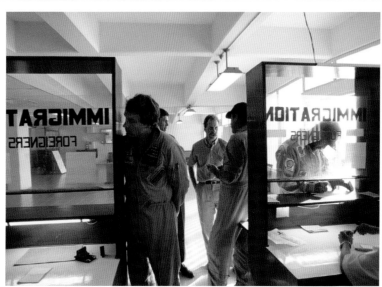
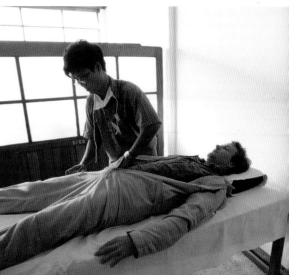

LEFT: The beautiful amber sunset belied an ominous feeling. The crew made this brief test flight above the Malaysian island of Langkawi after a jittery flight from Bangkok. Battling atrocious weather along the way, Peter and Lang had to scud along the top of the jungle, dodging huge limestone outcroppings, or "plugs," that often appeared in front of them out of the drizzly mist. Meanwhile, the right engine had developed a mild but uncontrollable oscillation, which forced the unscheduled stop at Langkawi.

RIGHT: Dan Nelson inspected the eroded end of a spark plug, the cause of unnerving sounds from the right engine as the Vimy crossed the Malay Peninsula. He improvised an effective fix by adapting an overly long motorcycle plug with extra washers.

BELOW: The Vimy broke ground for a test hop around Langkawi. Although performance was improved, the right engine was still down on power. The team had no choice but to push on to Singapore and better facilities.

Bands, schoolchildren, and a traditional dancing Chinese dragon for good luck greeted the Vimy at Seletar Airport in Singapore. The crew stayed for two days and made additional repairs after a second emergency landing, this time at Sitiawan, Malaysia, where they were lucky to find an overgrown Japanese base from World War II.

The Vimy bid farewell to the metropolis of Singapore on the morning of October 9, 1994, but the ailing biplane would need good wishes. As she crossed the equator, just south of Singapore, the groans from the starboard engine returned. Above Sumatra, the crew would confront not clear skies but dense smoke.

FAR LEFT: Eyes stinging after three hours of plowing through dense smoke, the pilots made a fuel stop in Palembang, Sumatra. The primitive island was enveloped end to end in smoke from uncontrolled fires set to clear the jungle. There was no choice but to refuel and head for Jakarta.

LEFT TOP: The tail of the aircraft was barely visible as the pilots plowed thorough the dense pall. The right engine warbled uncertainly. Peter turned the plane gently to the east toward the Java Sea in search of clear air in the hope of gaining precious altitude.

LEFT BOTTOM: Skimming just above the dense Sumatran jungle, the Vimy tried to reach the Java Sea about 30 miles to the east. At this point, the right engine was in its death rattle. Had it failed, the Vimy would have speared into the jungle in a fireball. "We dared not lose sight of the ground, but altitude was life," Peter recalled. "If she had quit when we were low, Jim, who was in the nose seat, would have been crushed, and I'm not sure we would have fared so well either. As we came closer to the sea, there were simply fewer trees to burn, the air was better, and we climbed. Every foot we gained gave us better options to choose a site to crash the plane."

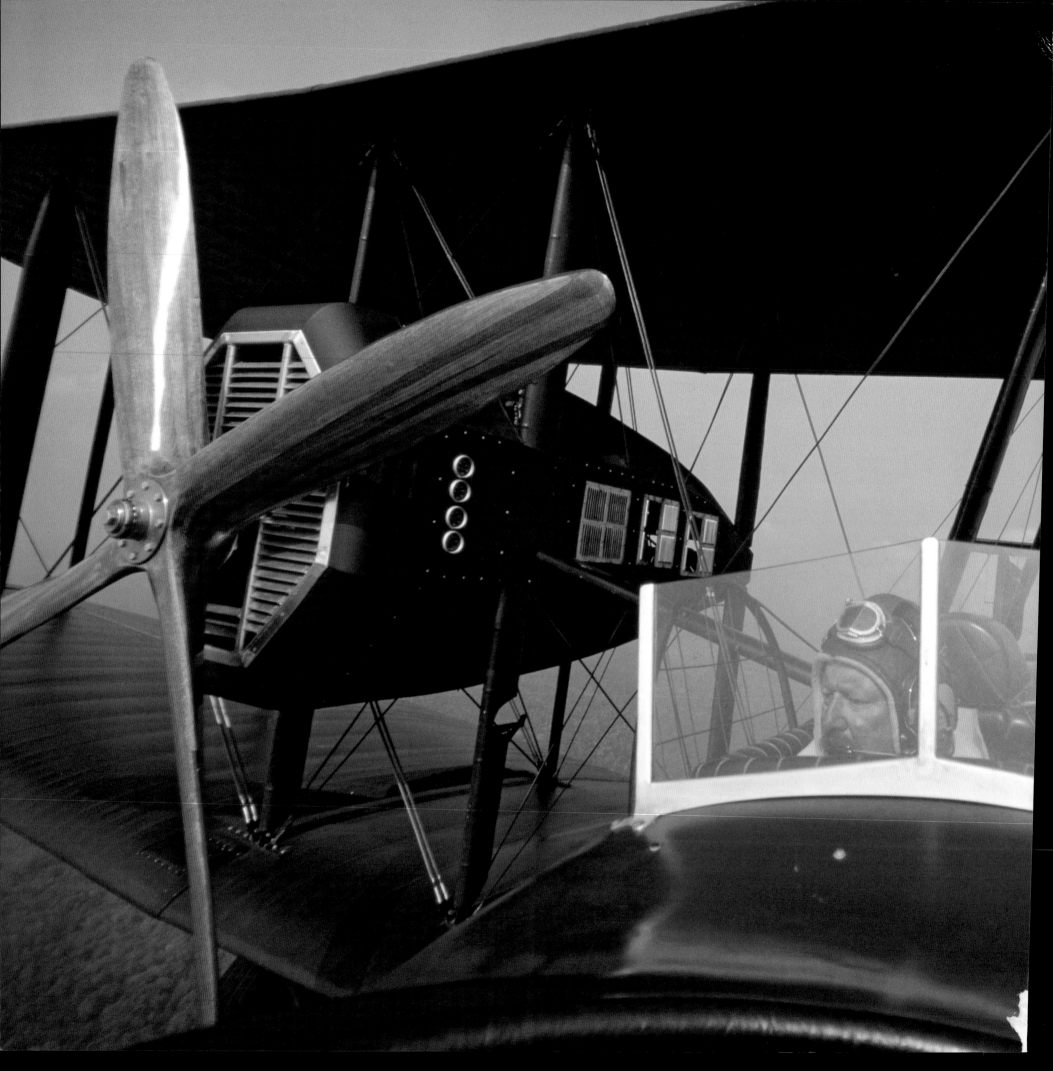

LEFT: Disaster struck on October 9 when the right engine quit at 3:12 p.m. over Talangbatu in Sumatra. Like a wounded bird, the Vimy started going down. Peter struggled to control the unwieldy aircraft while he and Lang desperately searched for a place to land. At least they had a few choices, the visibility had improved, and they had been able to climb to 1,800 feet. Jim Stanfield, captivated by the excitement of the moment, stood up in the nose to photograph the motionless right propeller. Peter yelled at him to sit and get his seatbelts on before the crash. Peter lined up to land in a burning rice field with tree stumps and a matrix of earth walls. The crew's prospects for survival seemed much better than in the hours before, but the rough field looked to be the end of the project.

TOP: Dan pulled off his life vest moments after the crash landing. Aside from the shattered engine, the Vimy had also broken her axles and tail wheel.

ABOVE: Hours after the crash, Mick Reynolds, piloting the Nomad, flew over the site in a gathering mist. Only the disembodied shape of the upper wing was visible: G-EAOU, truly God 'Elp All Of Us.

ABOVE: Shortly after Peter landed the Vimy in the Sumatran field, the area, which had appeared sparsely populated from the air, teemed with excitement. Hundreds of farmers and villagers, most of whom had never seen an airplane, pressed against the Vimy, drumming her flammable fabric, many holding cigarettes. Few had ever seen a full-bearded Caucasian like Dan Nelson (center with water bottle). When he walked away from the aircraft, most of the people followed him. This gave Peter, Lang, and Jim a chance to rope off the plane before it was incinerated by one of the smokers.

FAR LEFT: Six days after the crash, Lang attached the mended tail wheel, which had been torn from the Vimy on her violent landing in the field.

LEFT: Peter showed the signs of long days working in the field to build a runway for the Vimy to escape and resume her journey.

ABOVE RIGHT AND FAR RIGHT: The enterprising Indonesians turned the Vimy crash site into the largest tourist destination in Sumatra. Vendors of all descriptions set up stalls to serve the farmers who helped Lang build the runway as well as those who came to stare at the peculiar machine and the crazy men who had brought her there.

RIGHT: Lang was chief engineer of Kidby International Airfield, as this strip became known. He first marked the boundaries of the area that needed clearing and then began pulling out stumps with his bare hands.

FAR RIGHT CENTER AND BOTTOM: Many stumps were too large even for Lang, so he recruited oxen to handle the heavy lifting. By the third day after the crash, the airstrip was largely cleared and packed down. Lang had engineered a formidable achievement by driving the local people to help through a combination of wages, cajoling, small bribes (mostly baked goods), and leading by example.

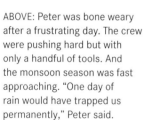

RIGHT: At 1740 hours on October 11, Mick Reynolds christened the freshly hacked-out airstrip. The Nomad's tires began to bog down in the spongy soil, but Mick quickly brought up the throttles and rolled to firmer ground. His fast actions saved the Australian government turboprop, which was not allowed to land on unpaved runways.

RIGHT BOTTOM, FROM LEFT: Peter and Mick Reynolds embraced just after the Nomad landed. Dan and Wayne Daley inspected the spare Vimy engine, which arrived in Jakarta four days after the crash. Five locals suspended the new engine, and Mick Reynolds, Bob Shaw (the Nomad engineer), and Lang guided it into place. Limited linguistic overlap made this a challenging feat.

ABOVE: Peter was bone weary after a frustrating day. The crew were pushing hard but with only a handful of tools. And the monsoon season was fast approaching. "One day of rain would have trapped us permanently," Peter said.

ABOVE RIGHT: Lang wiped his face after a few hours in the field. The atmosphere was indescribably dusty with smoke still hovering from the burning fields and jungles.

RIGHT: The team worked continuously in the days after the crash, but the tasks often seemed insurmountable. The heat and dust took a toll on morale by last light each day. The pungent smoke made it tough to breathe at all.

FAR RIGHT: Dan Nelson held the shattered bits of piston and piston rings destroyed by an exhaust valve. He pulled the engine apart with just small hand tools and found these fragments in the oil pan.

Six days after her crash landing in Sumatra, the Vimy had a new engine and a partially repaired undercarriage, and was well enough to try for Jakarta, about 180 miles away. Due to the heat and dust of Sumatra, the crew could only test-run the new engine for about eight minutes before giving her maximum power for takeoff.

Circling to gain height before heading out over the Java Sea, the Vimy bid adieu to the farmers and local officials who had worked tirelessly to make her well again. The Vimy crew helped finance the reconstruction of the bunds, the earthen walls that broke the plane's axles on landing and had to be flattened to make Kidby International Airfield.

The Vimy pushed eastward across the rugged islands of Indonesia. These legs involved a continuous battle with strong headwinds and turbulence. The aircraft averaged a ground speed of just over 50 miles per hour in traveling 800 miles from Jakarta to Timor. As the terrain indicates, there were no second chances in the event of another engine failure.

ABOVE: Jim Stanfield strapped himself into the struts behind the cockpit for this shot looking down on Kalijati, Indonesia. His feet are just visible at the bottom of the frame.

RIGHT: After the right engine quit above Sumatra, Peter and Lang frequently glanced out to the engine gauges on the side of the cowls.

FAR RIGHT TOP: Peter checked the fuel as the team prepared for the next leg. During the eight hours between Timor and Darwin, Australia, the Vimy would be flying over water.

FAR RIGHT BOTTOM: Dan Nelson looked hard at every wire and cable before the flight across the Timor Sea. "Peter and Lang were going on their own due to the full load of fuel," he said, "and none us would have ever let them down with a careless inspection."

A green strip in the distance heralded victory for the adventure. On many days in the prior two years, the outcome of the endeavor had been in doubt. "We saw only half a dozen boats over more than 400 miles of water," Lang told reporters in Darwin. "Lang had to concentrate on keeping the plane level. The horizon was so hazy it was disorienting," Peter added, "and there wasn't much map reading for me to handle!"

FAR LEFT: The sign said it all as the Vimy was captured a split second before touching down on Terra Australis, as Ross Smith referred to his home soil. "Reaching Darwin culminated all of our dreams and efforts," Peter said. The Vimy crew had endured much: foul weather, mechanical problems, red tape, and occasionally despair. But what better demonstration that the pioneering spirit lives on.

TOP LEFT: Dan jumped on board after touchdown in Darwin for a celebratory hug.

TOP RIGHT: Safely on the ground, Lang sipped Champagne, and Peter swigged from the magnum.

ABOVE LEFT: A ring gathered around the Vimy as Peter and Lang shared tales of their unusual tour.

ABOVE RIGHT: Peter and Lang paid homage to the Smith brothers, Wally Shiers, and Jim Bennett, as they stood on the site where the original Vimy G-EAOU touched down in Australia on December 10, 1919.

LEFT: The Vimy posed in front of her descendant, a Qantas Boeing 747. It seemed remarkable that only 50 years had passed between the 1919 flight of G-EAOU and the first commercial flight of the 747. Ross Smith, on arriving in Australia, said that the Vimy "represented the zenith of man's constructional genius."

The huge biplane seemed swallowed up in the vastness of the Australian Outback. Although the flights across the middle of Australia were long and often bumpy and cold, the terrain was flat and friendly. The pilots found the "inland sea" much preferable to the shark-infested Timor Sea.

The Vimy made a cloud of dust as she landed for a breakfast stop at Barkly Roadhouse, Northern Territory.

Erik Durfey took a photo of the Vimy and crew after breakfast in the Outback.

The flying machine stood near the hangar at Longreach, Queensland, where Qantas started in 1927.

Foul weather and high winds grounded the Vimy for a few days in Narromine, New South Wales.

On the victory lap through the Outback, the crew stopped at Cloncurry, Queensland.

The Vimy circled above the tropical coastal town of Coffs Harbour, New South Wales, before landing.

Howling winds kept the Vimy tied down at Mittagong, south of Sydney, for several days. A premature attempt to depart for Melbourne nearly ended in disaster. Even after 14,000 miles, she was still a primitive and temperamental flying machine.

TOP LEFT: Mark Rebholz offered an explanation to one of many queries from a future explorer. Mark and others from the Vimy crew spent countless hours spreading the spirit of adventure to curious youngsters.

LEFT: Mark cruised alongside the Vimy in a vintage Bellanca that he had flown from England to Australia in 1990.

TOP: Bill Whitney, designer of the re-created Vimy, helped instruct a would-be pilot in the cockpit.

ABOVE: The Vimy took off with another Bill Whitney creation, the full-scale replica of the Fokker Trimotor Southern Cross. It was the first plane to cross the Pacific Ocean from the United States to Australia, in 1926.

ABOVE: Peter and Lang gave a number of rides to Vimy enthusiasts in Adelaide. The team spent several days there as a finale in tribute to the Smith brothers, who came from a nearby sheep station.

RIGHT: The Vimy left one of the many small farms where she stopped on her way around Australia. "After weeks of jungles, expanses of water, and doubt," Peter said, "it was magical to be flying over flat, friendly terrain and then to land for good country fare."

Cruising down the east coast of
Australia between Coffs Harbour
and Port Macquarie, the Vimy crew
enjoyed views of the pristine beaches
and cobalt blue water.

The Original Vickers Vimy G-EAOU

G-EAOU was presented by Vickers Ltd. to the Australian government at the conclusion of the 1919 race. Although the race was meant to finish in Sydney, Ross and Keith Smith flew on to their hometown of Adelaide in South Australia. G-EAOU was declared unfit to fly by the authorities and was war weary in any case. She was shipped to Canberra and displayed there for many years, then was returned to Adelaide and placed in storage, where she was damaged in a fire in November 1957. Eventually, G-EAOU was restored to some degree and installed in a building at the Adelaide airport, where she resides to this day.

Lang and I, along with the Vimy crew, were delighted to have a close look at this historic machine despite her decrepit state. Inside many of the little wooden access doors along the nose of the fuselage, we found signatures and wishes of "bon voyage" dated October 1919, scrawled by the workers at the Vickers shop at Brooklands. "She looked tired," I said, "but we were spellbound thinking of what she had accomplished so long ago." As BBC reporter Rod Sharpe wrote, "One can imagine that late at night, when all the crews in Adelaide have gone home, the jumbo jets roll out of their hangars to gather round the Vimy and listen to her amazing stories."

TOP RIGHT: Flying across the Australian Outback involved long, cold legs often with turbulence, but each stop offered warm food and friendly greetings.

CENTER RIGHT: The Vimy left another sheep station, where the crew stopped for a breakfast of eggs and beans.

RIGHT: The Vimy cut the corner from Melbourne to Adelaide, through Mildura, Victoria.

FAR RIGHT: The legs became shorter as the Vimy team flew southward, but the team often battled bad weather. As had been the case in Europe, they could not go around or over the weather. Instead, they had to plow on and come out the other side soaking wet.

The Vimy made a triumphant lap past the Heads, over Sydney Harbour Bridge, and then back over the landmark Opera House. As the sun set on the expedition, the Vimy finished slightly bruised and dusty, her wings and wires splotched with oil, but she had cast her shadow over half the world.

Looking Toward Our Next Adventure

Our well-worn flying machine rested peacefully in a hangar at Kevin Weldon's farm, Luskintyre, in Australia's Hunter Valley. It was a pity for the Vimy to be gathering dust, but our epic adventure to Australia had left us with dry tanks, financially speaking. We held out hope that we could find a way to finance the two great flights that still awaited us.

Shilling by shilling, we scraped together small sponsorships to bring the Vimy back to the UK, where we could conduct flying displays that might attract major sponsorship for a flight to Africa. Lang Kidby, Erik Durfey, and I returned to Luskintyre. We pulled the Vimy to bits and packed her carefully into two 40-foot containers, noting a number of bent parts and bruises that would need to be repaired as she was reassembled in England.

The Vimy was airworthy again by 1996, but the project was always behind in funding. Through the efforts of Jenny Moseley, who ran *National Geographic*'s operations in the UK, and those of Matt Bresler, a business consultant turned Vimy volunteer, we gained enough support to begin considering the Africa flight. Peter McBride joined the team, performing tasks of all descriptions, including building Vimy models with logo mock-ups for various prospective sponsors. Our advance person, Catherine Sellman, journeyed to South Africa in search of local patrons. She was welcomed by the van Ryneveld family, whose ancestor, Pierre van Ryneveld, had piloted one of the Vimys competing in the original 1920 race from England to Africa.

As part of our planning, we contemplated a necessary but costly change of engines. We needed more power for the high terrain and vast distances of East Africa. Eventually BMW offered to supply customized engines, but the cost of adapting and installing them set us back another two years. John LaNoue moved to England to complete these formidable tasks. Finally, by the fall of 1998, we had an operable machine again. We painted her bright silver in homage to her 1920 ancestor, the *Silver Queen*.

As we looked ahead to Africa, our experience in Australia led us to expect delays due to weather, mechanical glitches, border conflicts, and bureaucratic intransigence. We also expected that the glory of Africa and the warmth of new friends met along the way would prevail over the inevitable setbacks and frictions. Perhaps that is the magnetic appeal of such adventures, compared to our everyday existence. We truly didn't know what would happen next. As the Vimy team took to saying, "We need to have a plan so at least we'll know what's not going to happen."

{ 1920 | 1999 }

England to South Africa

Queen of the African Skies

Soaring over Masai Mara National Park and enjoying open, unrestricted airspace in Kenya, the Vimy lined up with the wildebeest migration.

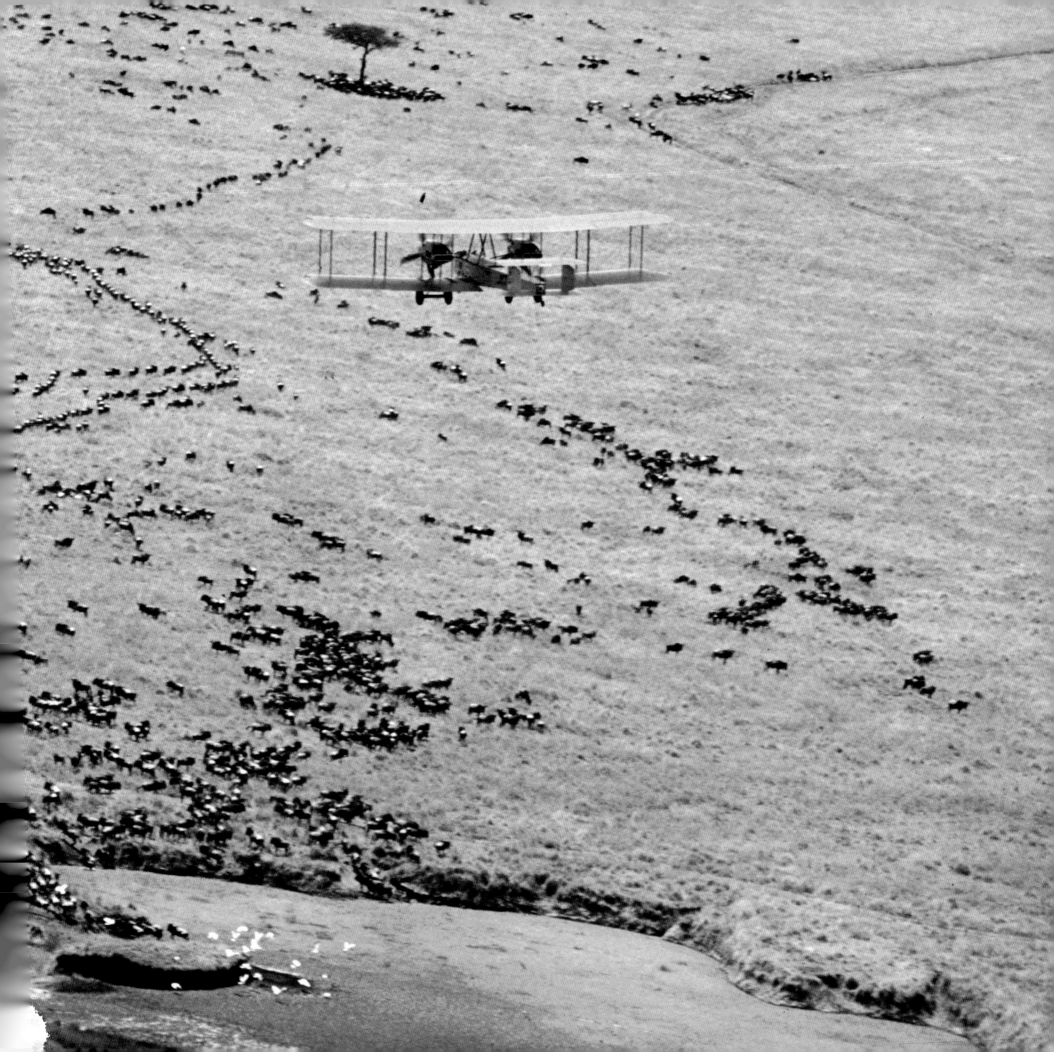

The Race for the Cape

by Peter McMillan The success of the transatlantic flight of June 1919 and the Smith brothers' epic at the end of that year convinced those airmen considering entry into the *Daily Mail* Race for the Cape that the Vickers Vimy would be the mount of choice. However, the African continent would offer different sorts of challenges. Despite their skills, determination, and bravery, the pilots of this event would leave behind splintered wood and torn fabric—four Vimys were destroyed by crashes along the way.

In 1920 the surveys of East Africa were still crude. Only a few small outposts had communication, and none had airfields. After all, it had been only 50 years since Henry Morton Stanley had found David Livingstone on the shores of Lake Tanganyika. Even more threatening than the remoteness of the Dark Continent was the fact that most of the route to the Cape was very hot and very high in elevation, obstacles that would prove to overwhelm the capabilities of the 1920 flying machines.

Fighting the African Sun

First to depart Brooklands, on January 24, 1920, was the Vimy Commercial model, registered G-EAAV. This entry, sponsored by the *London Times,* was ably manned in the cockpit by Captain Stanley Cockerell, the chief test pilot for Vickers, and Captain F. C. Broome. In the cabin were two mechanics, Sergeant Major James Wyatt and C. Corby. Also on board was an eminent zoologist, Dr. Peter Chalmers Mitchell. The flight aimed to make scientific discoveries as well as the first aerial survey of Africa.

The first phase of the flight was uneventful, with ports of call at Marseilles, Rome, Malta, and Benghazi in what is now Libya before alighting at Heliopolis, near Cairo, where they would make detailed preparations for the trek to Cape Town, nearly 5,000 miles away. G-EAAV lifted off early

FAR LEFT: The South African government provided a Vimy to Pierre van Ryneveld (left) and C. J. Quintin Brand (right). The South African pilots were accompanied by two mechanics. The aircraft also carried plenty of spare parts.

LEFT: The *Silver Queen*, bearing the registration G-UABA, was fueled for the race as she stood on the compass turntable at Brooklands. The aircraft had a fuel capacity of more than 500 gallons. Van Ryneveld and Brand departed at 7:30 a.m. on February 4 and headed for Turin, Italy.

TOP: Stanley Cockerell and F. C. Broome were the first to leave Brooklands. Their Vimy Commercial reached Egypt without incident. After that, they were beset by successive mechanical problems. The plane crashed in Tabora, Tanganyika, and was beyond repair.

ABOVE: Van Ryneveld and Brand hoped to fly directly from Cairo to Khartoum. They wrote off the *Silver Queen* after an emergency landing at Wadi Halfa in Sudan but were able to salvage the engines and have them installed in a new Vimy airframe.

TOP: Now piloting the *Silver Queen II*, powered by the engines from their first Vimy, van Ryneveld and Brand departed Egypt on February 22. They reached Ndola in Zambia on March 1, having been delayed by stops for engine repairs.

ABOVE: After waiting out two days of bad weather, van Ryneveld and Brand left Ndola for the short flight to Broken Hill (present-day Kabwe) and an opportunity to refuel.

TOP RIGHT: A crowd surrounded the *Silver Queen II* when she arrived in Bulawayo on March 5.

on February 5 but was soon suffering from heat in the form of extreme turbulence. The left engine overheated, forcing a rapid landing in the desert outside Luxor, Egypt. Inspection revealed that the water jackets surrounding each of the cylinders had small cracks that allowed most of the cooling liquid to leak away. The mechanics commenced repairs with soap and tape, while local Egyptian farmers were sent to the Nile to obtain water. Aswan was reached before dark on the night of February 5. The crew spent the next day making additional fixes.

Over the next 21 days, G-EAAV made more than 10 additional forced landings, most due to leaking water and overheating engines. The aircraft suffered a variety of other problems, including faulty magnetos, which reduced or sometimes cut off the ignition to one engine or the other. Cables were slackened by the turbulence and extreme temperatures. Some of the mishaps occurred in impossibly remote locations several days' walk from any resources. As a result, the crew could make only crude repairs and limp to a location closer to a water source and some form of civilization. The heat, altitude, and dust of Africa were causing the engines and the airplane to erode by the hour.

Harsh conditions often required the crew to offload all but minimum fuel to reach a reasonable location where they could complete repairs. Thus, G-EAAV was obliged on several occasions to take on local gasoline that was suspect, rather than use the stores that had been deposited for them.

The aircraft blew a tire on a forced landing in Uganda. More than 2,000 miles remained to the Cape.

The end came at Tabora in Tanganyika (present-day Tanzania). On takeoff early in the morning, a fountain of water erupted from the right engine, and Cockerell brought the Vimy back for an immediate landing. After three hours of repairs, the crew made another attempt to take off around 2 p.m., in the heat of the day. Just after the aircraft left the ground, the right engine went silent. The Vimy had no hope of climbing and quickly returned to earth, crashing into stumps and scrubby trees. The wheels smashed up through the lower wings. The Vimy was shredded. Fortunately, the crew's injuries were minor.

The Silver Queen Takes Off

The next contestant was the Vimy (bomber version) sponsored by the South African government and dubbed the *Silver Queen*. The name was inspired by the dope mixed with aluminum powder painted on the Vimy's Irish linen covering to reflect the harsh African sun.

The *Silver Queen* was manned by South African pilots Lieutenant Colonel Pierre van Ryneveld and Major C. J. Quintin Brand along with their mechanics. She departed Brooklands on February 4, 1920, and two days later achieved a spectacular success by flying nonstop for 14 hours from Taranto in the heel of Italy all the way to Sollum in Libya.

From Cairo, van Ryneveld planned to travel only at night, hoping to avoid the heat-related problems attendant to flying in Africa during daytime. They had to make Khartoum in Sudan, 1,000 miles to the south, by the night of February 19. But a radiator leak necessitated landing at 5 a.m. in near total darkness. What may have looked like a smooth landing site in the desert proved otherwise. Shortly after touching down, the *Silver Queen* lay smashed among boulders. Miraculously, the four crewmen were unhurt. The South African attempt appeared to have died then and there, along the Nile about 500 miles south of Cairo. But the hardy South Africans would not be denied their chance for the glory of being the first men to fly home to the Cape.

As a start, the engines of the *Silver Queen* were salvageable. The South African government arranged with the Royal Air Force in Cairo to make another Vimy available for a second attempt. The engines and instruments were removed from the wreckage and floated down the Nile to Cairo. By February 22, they had been installed in the *Silver Queen II,* and the South Africans were ready to get under way again. After reaching Khartoum a day later, they made excellent progress for 1,000 miles to Mongalla in Sudan and then to Shirati in Tanganyika with only minor problems, including leaking water jackets and scraping the top of a tree with the lower wing when flying over a landing spot to chase away animals.

Near Tragedy Close to Home

On February 28 the *Silver Queen II* passed over Tabora and the crash site of G-EAAV. Entering Northern Rhodesia (present-day Zambia), where the highest continuous terrain averages more than a mile above sea level, they shed as much gear as possible at Abercorn (now known as Mbala).

On the next leg, reduced power, resulting from an ignition problem, left the crew gently floating downward, but they managed to make Ndola, only 1,500 miles from home. After a series of short hops due to the need to carry light fuel loads across the heights and to delays from torrential rainstorms, they arrived in Bulawayo, Southern Rhodesia (present-day Zimbabwe), on March 5. Along the way, they had taken the first aerial photos of Victoria Falls.

Perhaps it was homesickness that persuaded van Ryneveld and Brand to take on enough fuel to fly to Pretoria, in their home country of South Africa. They bravely launched from Bulawayo. The takeoff went well, but the heat, the height, the weight, and perhaps an ignition fault were too much for the old girl to climb away. *Silver Queen II* made a tangled wreckage a mile from the airfield.

Refusing to be stopped, they prevailed upon the South African government to deliver a small de Havilland D.H.9 biplane to Bulawayo two weeks later. Van Ryneveld and Brand then flew the last 1,300 miles home, even though their change of craft made them ineligible for the *Daily Mail* prize. They arrived in Cape Town as national heroes on March 20, 1920, and were lauded for their bravery and for their sheer persistence.

Once at Bulawayo, van Ryneveld and Brand were just over 1,300 miles from Cape Town. The next day, they aimed to fly the 400 miles from Bulawayo to Pretoria without stopping. Due to an engine malfunction, the *Silver Queen II* was unable to remain aloft. Though the crew survived, the plane could not be salvaged.

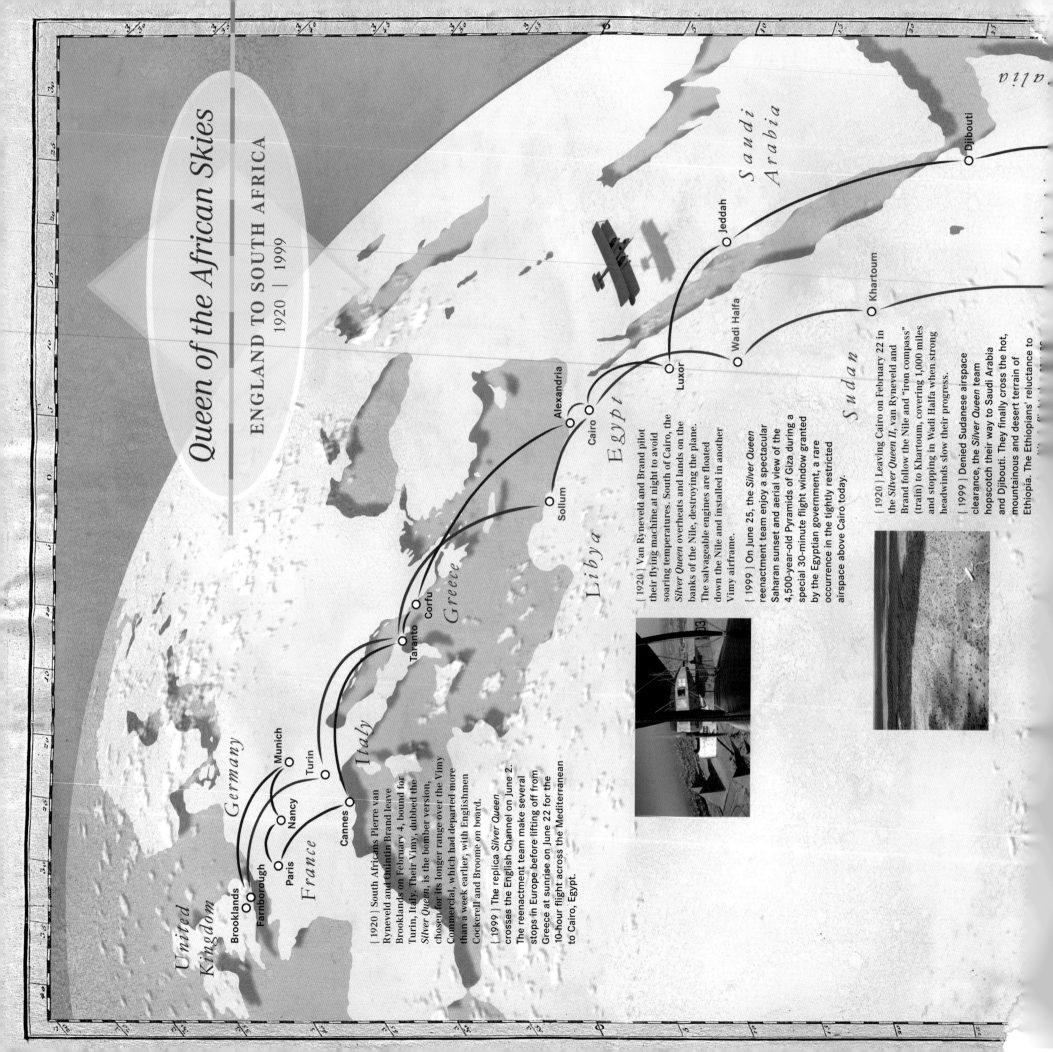

Queen of the African Skies

ENGLAND TO SOUTH AFRICA
1920 | 1999

United Kingdom

Germany

Munich

Turin

Nancy

Paris

Farnborough

Brooklands

France

Italy

Cannes

Taranto

Corfu

Greece

Sollum

Alexandria

Cairo

Egypt

Libya

Luxor

Wadi Halfa

Jeddah

Saudi Arabia

Khartoum

Sudan

Djibouti

{ 1920 } South Africans Pierre van Ryneveld and Quintin Brand leave Brooklands on February 4, bound for Turin, Italy. Their *Vimy*, dubbed the *Silver Queen*, is the bomber version, chosen for its longer range over the *Vimy Commercial*, which had departed more than a week earlier, with Englishmen Cockerell and Broome on board.

{ 1999 } The replica *Silver Queen* crosses the English Channel on June 2. The reenactment team make several stops in Europe before lifting off from Greece at sunrise on June 22 for the 10-hour flight across the Mediterranean to Cairo, Egypt.

{ 1920 } Van Ryneveld and Brand pilot their flying machine at night to avoid soaring temperatures. South of Cairo, the *Silver Queen* overheats and lands on the banks of the Nile, destroying the plane. The salvageable engines are floated down the Nile and installed in another *Vimy* airframe.

{ 1999 } On June 25, the *Silver Queen* reenactment team enjoy a spectacular Saharan sunset and aerial view of the 4,500-year-old Pyramids of Giza during a special 30-minute flight window granted by the Egyptian government, a rare occurrence in the tightly restricted airspace above Cairo today.

{ 1920 } Leaving Cairo on February 22 in the *Silver Queen II*, van Ryneveld and Brand follow the Nile and "iron compass" (train) to Khartoum, covering 1,000 miles and stopping in Wadi Halfa when strong headwinds slow their progress.

{ 1999 } Denied Sudanese airspace clearance, the *Silver Queen* team hopscotch their way to Saudi Arabia and Djibouti. They finally cross the hot, mountainous and desert terrain of Ethiopia. The Ethiopians' reluctance to

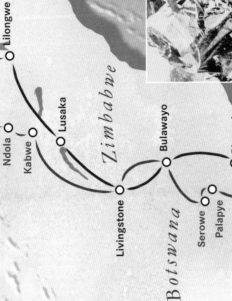

1920 Expedition

1999 Expedition

Tanzania

Malawi

Zambia

Zimbabwe

Botswana

South Africa

Kisumu · Nairobi · Chyulu Hills · Shirati · Arusha · Dodoma · Mbeya · Lilongwe · Mbala · Ndola · Kabwe · Lusaka · Livingstone · Bulawayo · Pietersburg · Pretoria · Johannesburg · Serowe · Palapye · Bloemfontein · Beaufort West · Cape Town

...wingtip of the *Silver Queen II* on treetops when attempting to scare off wildlife from the runway in Tanzania. They manage to avoided crashing.

[1999] For a spectacular morning photo flight on July 19, the Vimy claws its way to 13,000 feet to see the snows of Mt. Kilimanjaro. Upon returning, the aircraft catches an unexpected crosswind, causing the wingtip to drag on landing in the remote Chyulu Hills of Kenya and narrowly avoiding disaster.

[1920] Flying mostly at night and as quickly as possible, the South Africans make a limited number of stops. At each one, they are received with interest and enthusiasm, as many Africans had never seen a flying machine.

[1999] Shortly after the Vimy makes an unannounced landing in Mbeya, Tanzania, hundreds of exuberant children surround the aircraft, curious to touch it and learn where the "time machine" came from. The excited welcome made the team feel as if the Vimy was the first plane to arrive on the remote runway.

[1920] Sensing a potential victory, the South Africans depart Bulawayo to cheering crowds. Topped off with fuel, the Vimy is unwilling to climb and the Vimy crashes east of the runway. The aircraft is totaled, but the crew and a cat, their mascot, escape with minor injuries.

[1999] Delayed by more than two weeks, the *Silver Queen* team lands at dusk on July 24 in Bulawayo to a crowd of thousands. Flashes pop and marching bands trumpet in a celebration organized by dedicated Bulawayo Vimy supporters. It is the largest welcome on the flight, and most likely similar to what van Ryneveld and Brand experienced upon their arrival.

[1920] Van Ryneveld and Brand complete the flight with the single-engine *Voortrekker*. The aviators cannot collect the *Daily Mail* prize but become the first pilots to open the African air passage, earning them a place in South African aviation history.

[1999] After toiling through turbulence, soaring heat, high altitude, and relentless red tape, the reenactment team reaches Cape Town on July 29. The *Silver Queen* replica becomes the first Vickers Vimy to wing its way over Table Mountain and the coastline. A local newspaper headline reads, "Vimy Finally Reaches Cape Town!"

Queen of the African Skies

by Peter McBride June 1, 1999, Brooklands, England. After two years of scraping together funds, we were prepared to follow the South Africans' route down the length of Africa. Mary Brand, the daughter of *Silver Queen* pilot Sir Christopher Quintin Brand, wished us well as we left Brooklands, her father's point of departure 79 years earlier. "Thank you for keeping a wonderful era alive," she said.

At 500 feet above the white-capped English Channel, rain danced on the Vimy's wings and stung our faces. Our craft heaved in the low clouds and buffeting winds. Serving as the flight's photographer, I was in the nose gunner's seat. Behind me, wedged shoulder to shoulder in the cockpit, were chief pilot Mark Rebholz and copilot John LaNoue. Peter McMillan, still working to pay off bills accumulated since the start of the project, had to remain behind.

The UK's Manston radar advised, "Mike Yankee [our call sign], you are now leaving our area." The voice came again, "Mike Yankee, I understand you are the Vickers Vimy. Is that correct?"

"Affirmative. We are en route to Cape Town," Mark replied.

"Brilliant!" The radio crackled with emotion rarely heard from air traffic controllers. "Best of luck, and Godspeed!"

Cruising at 75 miles per hour, the *Silver Queen* would take more than 30 hours of flying through Europe to reach Africa. We carried electronics and detailed maps that our predecessors didn't have, but we still had to cross 11 countries and two war zones and contend with bush airfields, mountains, limited fuel access, and winter in the Southern Hemisphere. We probably needed that "Godspeed" after all.

Our first hop to Munich was followed by a short fueling stop in Nancy, France. But the French authorities had a different agenda. The flying machine, impounded for "customs violations," quickly became a jailbird. A few exasperating days and $3,000 later, she was freed on bail. Financially lightened, we motored on through France, then down Italy. Before sunrise on June 22, we lifted off from Greece and headed to Africa—a mere 10-hour flight across the Mediterranean. Wind keened in the Vimy's 114 bracing wires, and her twin 360-horsepower BMW engines churned out their deafening drone.

The Hardest Leg

Untangling aviation red tape often proved more challenging than navigation. In Egypt we discovered that there was more interest in charging elevated landing fees because the Vimy was "unique" than there was

DEPARTURE: June 1, 1999; Brooklands, England

ARRIVAL: July 29, 1999; Cape Town, South Africa

DURATION: 58 days and 9,082 miles

PILOTS: Mark Rebholz and John LaNoue

SUPPORT CREW: Matt Bresler, Mick Follari, Jenny Moseley, Patty Rebholz, Leah Wingfield

After liftoff from England, the Vimy weathered 4,000 miles of flying at high elevations, in hot temperatures, and through tense airspaces. By comparison, braving a storm on the remote, acacia-lined runway at Samburo National Park in Kenya was a welcome reprieve.

curiosity about the project. Nevertheless, on June 25 we flew over the pyramids of Giza during a short flight clearance to take photos. We encountered larger doses of hospitality away from the runways when we took a day to ride horses into the Sahara around the pyramids. But time and money were limited, so we pushed on.

Denied clearance by Sudan, we had to divert to the east of the original 1920 route, but before leaving Egypt, John cut away much of the engine cowlings to help cool the engines in the soaring Saharan temperatures. Upon landing in Jeddah, Saudi Arabia, we made more mechanical adjustments. Fortunately, fixing an oil leak took a day. The delay allowed us to plan another new route, some nine hours down the Red Sea through Yemen's airspace, in order to avoid the Ethiopian jets that were bombing Eritrea (two weeks later, a British Lear jet was shot down by the Ethiopian fighters for "flying off its flight plan").

Relieved after averting potential danger, we were welcomed into Djibouti with an intercept by two French Mirage jets. Having had only one radio warning from the Djiboutian tower—and none from the unidentified jet pilots—we were at first uncertain of our company in the hazy skies over the Red Sea. After two passes, Mark detected, by their flying skills, that they were likely French. Once on the ground in Djibouti, we met the pilots, French indeed, who told us how upon seeing the Vimy, they thought they had flown "through a time warp."

Unable to rouse air traffic controllers and possessing an expired flight clearance, Mark and John took off from Djibouti on July 4, banking south toward Ethiopia in a hazy headwind. It wasn't quite dawn, and the temperature was already 90° Fahrenheit. Heavy fighting between Ethiopia and Somalia had dominated preflight discussions, with anxious talk of forced landings, hostage situations, and roads full of trigger-happy soldiers. To allow more fuel onboard, I traveled ahead commercially to Nairobi, Kenya, hoping luck would blow south. It didn't. The Vimy reached only 8,800 feet and covered less than 200 ground miles in four hours. Exhausted by arm-straining turbulence and relentless headwinds, Mark and John turned back. A week of faxes and sleepless nights later, they secured a flight clearance for July 12.

I returned to Djibouti with Mark Garland, a Kenyan pilot. The two of us would ferry extra fuel and, with the aid of Iain Douglas-Hamilton, offer support with wind updates as we motored ahead to the Kenyan border in a twin-engine Aztec. Dodging headwinds, the *Silver Queen* managed to cross Ethiopia and landed at Mandera in Kenya, a journey of eight numbing hours. Mark Rebholz called it "the most demanding flight of my career."

Panorama of Kenya

"You are making history," said a grinning army officer, gesturing at the only airworthy Vickers Vimy in the world, parked on his isolated base in northern Kenya. Word of our arrival had spread quickly through Mandera, a predominantly Muslim hamlet tight against the Somalia-Ethiopia border. That night, local pilots shared their modest accommodations with us.

At five the next morning, we found schoolgirls in billowing purple uniforms waiting by the *Silver Queen*, notepads poised, eager to learn about

what they called our "time machine." "We have heard of the Wright brothers," one said, "but what is this, and why are you here?" Mark responded with an impromptu aviation tutorial.

Dodging storks and potholes on takeoff from Mandera, we flew eight and a half hours to Nairobi's Wilson Airport. Despite being two weeks overdue, we were met by cheering crowds. The expedition's education team joined us in Nairobi. Selected in an essay contest, five students from five countries—the youngest 14 years old, the oldest 18—followed the flight on the ground from Kenya to South Africa, led by tutors Mick Follari and Matt Bresler. Miriam Alube, an 18-year-old Kenyan, was the first student to go up in the *Silver Queen*. She landed crying, overwhelmed by seeing her home from an open cockpit for the first time.

After crossing the Great Rift Valley, we joined friends and supporters at Iain and Oria Douglas-Hamilton's farm by Lake Naivasha for an evening of classic bush hospitality. But our two-week delay in Djibouti left us little time to relax. The next morning, we set off again for a photo flight with scores of waving hands urging us skyward. Saluting another large and improbable creature, the Vimy dipped a wing to the elephants grazing on the golden plains of the Masai Mara game reserve. With the stress of crossing war-torn Ethiopia behind us, we reveled in peaceful flying. Zebras, gazelles, and wildebeests roamed just a thousand feet below.

We had no trouble with the engines overheating ever since John cut away large pieces of their cowlings in Egypt, but we still faced the challenge of Kenya's high elevations. Taking off from central Kenya on July 16 and again testing the *Silver Queen*'s limitations, we were reminded that every flight is a test flight. Weighted with fuel, she refused to climb in the thin air above a high-elevation runway. Skirting treetops, Mark waited for fuel to burn off and noted in his log: "Too heavy if any obstacles."

Three hours later, we touched down on a grass airstrip in the Chyulu Hills in Kenya, just north of Tanzania. Apprehensive Masai examined us from a distance, then, despite language barriers, were quickly fascinated by our craft. One drummed gleefully on her fabric-covered fuselage.

A Beautiful View, Followed by Near Disaster

On July 19, before leaving Kenya, Mark and John detoured to Tanzania and pushed the *Silver Queen* to 13,000 feet in the cooler air of snow-capped Mt. Kilimanjaro and were rewarded with a dazzling view of Africa's highest peak. I photographed the spectacle from Richard Bonham's Cessna 206. Richard kindly shared his Chyulu Hills camp and aircraft to help. And, of course, help we needed.

On the *Silver Queen*'s return, a crosswind caught her wings and John off guard. Despite both pilots' quick reactions on the heavy controls, the starboard wing gouged into the dirt runway. I watched in disbelief from the ground, my camera drive whirling as the Vimy skirted total disaster. "We almost cartwheeled and rolled up into a ball," Mark said, slumping in exhausted frustration. We assessed the damage: a bent aileron control and another delay. We could not afford to repeat our predecessors' misadventures. Van Ryneveld and Brand wrecked two Vimys and finished their journey in a borrowed D.H.9. There would be no second

FAR LEFT: Embarking from Brooklands, England, on June 1, the Vimy began its hopscotch flight plan through Europe en route to Africa.

TOP LEFT: Chief pilot Mark Rebholz (right) shared a smile with Dizzy Addicott, a Vickers Vimy test pilot.

TOP RIGHT: Mary Brand, daughter of 1920 Vimy pilot Quintin Brand, inspected the replica before liftoff.

ABOVE LEFT: Vimy builder and pilot John LaNoue waited out a storm at La Ferté-Alais, France.

ABOVE: An aspiring pilot posed in front of the Vimy after its first leg to Munich, Germany, seven and a half hours through rain and fog.

Vimy for us, and if a quick repair weren't possible, Mark would run out of leave from his job and have to abandon the flight. Mark and John, exhausted to the bone and their morale low, headed back to Nairobi in Richard Bonham's Cessna, hoping to find parts and locate fuel for the rest of the trip. I stayed behind to secure our battered *Silver Queen*.

Eight hours later, John returned, parts in hand. After another night of Kenyan hospitality at the Bonhams' isolated camp, John and I walked three hours back to the airfield. Giraffes and antelope eyed us as we waded through tick-infested grasses crisscrossed by lion tracks. With more ingenuity than equipment, John revived the plane he built. Meanwhile, having learned via telephone of a fuel cache in southern Tanzania, Mark rejoined us on July 21, thanks to another friendly pilot who offered a ride. Spirits lifting, we continued our southward journey.

Completing the Race for the Cape

As we crossed Tanzania's forests, scattered smoke plumes were the sole signs of habitation. Turning on to a grass landing strip in Mbeya, we expected to find only a missionary pilot and his personal fuel reserve. But before our 11-foot propellers stopped whirling, hundreds of children and adults poured onto the field, encircling the *Silver Queen* with Swahili cheers and toothy grins. Their enthusiasm buoyed us through three days of dawn-to-dusk flying over Malawi and Zambia. The effort sapped our bodies but offered rewards we did not anticipate. On July 24 we soared across the earth-splitting Victoria Falls at the very spot where in 1920 Quintin Brand made the first aerial photograph of the 354-foot chasm.

From the Zambezi River and the falls, we raced through western Zimbabwe, the sun on our tail. On the evening of July 24, we touched down at Bulawayo International Airport. Marching bands and more than 2,000 well-wishers saluted us, cameras flashing and Champagne corks popping. Some in the crowd remembered seeing the *Silver Queen* cut through the sky 79 years before. Unlike van Ryneveld and Brand, who were keen to complete their African air race, we took in the Zimbabwean hospitality and stayed for a day. When we departed, we cautiously left with lighter tanks, hoping not to repeat the fate of our predecessors, who crashed shortly after takeoff.

Grimy and worn, we sprinted across South Africa in subfreezing winter weather. As we neared our goal, rain, hail, and snow slashed our faces, but the *Silver Queen* persevered. On July 29 we at last swept across the shores of Cape Town and touched down at Cape Town International Airport, becoming the first Vimy to soar over South Africa. The headlines the next day read, "Vimy Finally Reaches Cape Town."

As John, Mark, and I discovered, air travel 1920 style offered few comforts. Fifty-eight days after leaving England, we arrived in Cape Town wearing the same clothes, deaf and hungry, with distended bladders and windburned faces. Yet flying in the Vimy's open cockpits gave us an intimate experience of eastern Africa's peoples and landscapes that few have shared. "My dear fellows," Pierre van Ryneveld said in a radio interview years after his flight, "if you had been a millionaire, you could not buy an adventure like that."

The Vimy battled fierce wind and rain on the way to France across the English Channel.

LEFT: The *Silver Queen* touched down at the antique French airfield of La Ferté-Alais south of Paris and the location of a well-known air show.

BOTTOM LEFT: The grass tarmac and collection of time machines at La Ferté-Alais were visible from the rear cockpit.

BOTTOM RIGHT: The Vimy wasn't always greeted by smiling spectators. After the crew touched down in Nancy, France, authorities impounded the plane and imposed a fine for customs violations.

RIGHT TOP: Chief pilot Mark Rebholz (left) drew on his 20,000 hours of professional flying experience to fly the Vimy through Africa. John LaNoue (center), copilot and builder of the re-created Vimy, maintained the aircraft for 9,000 miles. Peter McBride (right), photographer and writer, documented the 58-day journey.

RIGHT: Seen from a tail-mounted camera, the 114 bracing wires shimmered as the *Silver Queen* departed La Ferté-Alais and banked south for her next stop, Cannes, France.

Mark and John were outfitted in life jackets for the flight over the Mediterranean to Taranto, Italy. Shoulder to shoulder in these cozy quarters, they manned the controls for some 150 hours to South Africa.

Due to military airspace restrictions, the *Silver Queen* was forced
to fly the entire western coast of Italy, including the Italian Riviera,
shown here, at under 1,000 feet. The Vimy is large and slow, which
created the impression that the world was gradually unrolling.
This gave the crew plenty of time to see and even smell the sights.

FAR LEFT: Lifting off at dawn from the island of Corfu, Greece, the *Silver Queen* reenacted the first nonstop Mediterranean crossing of van Ryneveld and Brand, who completed the leg in 14 hours at night in 1920.

ABOVE LEFT: After flying nearly 10 hours by daylight, the *Silver Queen* reached the shores of Alexandria, Egypt. While the street vendors proved friendly, airport officials were less so, demanding high landing fees and strict flight clearances.

ABOVE RIGHT: Whenever the Vimy crossed bodies of water such as the Mediterranean, Peter rode in the rear armed with both a life raft and an emergency locater device.

LEFT: The view from the air underscored the stark contrast between the irrigated land of the Nile Delta and the sands of the Sahara Desert.

TOP: A family in Giza talked about the "flying kite" they saw circle their historic backyard the previous day.

ABOVE: An Egyptian television crew interviewed John at the Embaba Airport in Cairo. Local media took interest in the Vimy's journey from Egypt to South Africa.

RIGHT: For 30 minutes during a Saharan sunset, the Egyptian authorities allowed the Vimy to circle the pyramids of Giza, thanks to the connections made with the Egyptian glider club.

LEFT: John and Mark contemplated the daunting task of redirecting their flight plan to Saudi Arabia and Djibouti, to avoid an unwelcoming Sudan.

OPPOSITE: After a day in Luxor, the Vimy veered from the 1920 route by leaving Africa and flying over the Red Sea to find fuel and friendly airspace in Jeddah, Saudi Arabia.

FAR LEFT TOP: Departing Jeddah at dawn with full tanks, the Vimy struggled to gain altitude for the first hour of a lumbering nine-hour leg through hazy skies over the Red Sea. During one of John's flying breaks, he rested his back.

LEFT: The Vimy skirted the conflict between Ethiopia and Eritrea by crossing Yemeni airspace before turning west to land in Djibouti. On the way, two French Mirage jets intercepted the aircraft (bottom). The French fighter pilots later befriended the Vimy crew (top).

FAR LEFT BOTTOM: In the 110° Fahrenheit heat of sunset in Djibouti, Mark and John pumped aviation gas in preparation for the flight across Ethiopia. Obtaining a low-altitude permit to cross Ethiopia proved harder than the flight itself, which involved straining the aircraft to haul full tanks over 8,000-foot mountain ranges.

TOP: The sun-baked streets of Djibouti became home for the crew for two weeks as the team tried to obtain a flight clearance to cross Ethiopia.

ABOVE: Mark Rebholz was helped by Kenyan pilot Mark Garland, who flew a support plane on the Vimy's second attempt to cross Ethiopia.

ABOVE RIGHT: A Djiboutian woman watched the Vimy crew at the airfield in the midsummer 120° Fahrenheit heat. Djiboutians joked that vehicle exhaust served as air conditioning.

RIGHT: The delay in Djibouti strained the Vimy's fabric and control cables. The French Air Force offered logistical support and a much-needed bath.

FAR RIGHT: Mark and John took off from Djibouti on July 4, heading south toward Ethiopia. Turbulence and headwinds forced them to return. They made this second attempt eight days later.

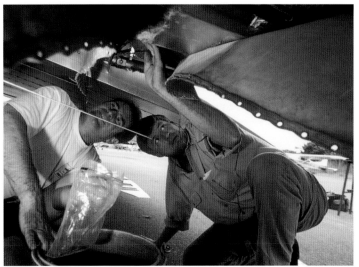

LEFT: Before the Vimy went to Mandera in Kenya, a UN pilot advised avoiding the town, "as people like to shoot at planes." The crew found only support and curiosity, including these schoolgirls.

TOP: While Mark and John struggled to cross Ethiopia, supporters at the Aero Club of East Africa in Nairobi, Kenya, tried to keep aviation enthusiasts informed of the progress.

ABOVE CENTER: Two weeks late and layered in dust, the Vimy and her crew reached Nairobi's Wilson Airport.

ABOVE: Mark and John repaired clogged fuel filters as volunteers helped clean the plane.

FAR LEFT TOP: Supporters cheered the aviators at the home of Iain and Oria Douglas-Hamilton on the shores of Lake Naivasha in Kenya.

FAR LEFT BOTTOM: At the Aero Club of East Africa in Nairobi, Mark spent hours plotting the remainder of the Africa legs. Famous aviators such as Beryl Markham frequented the club.

ABOVE: In Naivasha, Mark and John shared tales of North African flying.

LEFT CENTER: Iain Douglas-Hamilton, elephant researcher, on his grass runway near Lake Naivasha, donated a week of flights in his Cessna 185 so Peter could take photos.

LEFT: Young Naivasha children giggled when they saw the giant flying machine.

RIGHT: After two weeks of delay and red tape in Djibouti, the open skies over Lake Naivasha were a welcome sight.

ABOVE: Due to the delays in crossing Ethiopia, the crew had little time to linger. A day after arriving at Lake Naivasha, the team pushed on from the Douglas-Hamilton farm to explore Kenya.

LEFT: Locals heard of the Vimy's arrival and created crowds on the grass tarmac at the Douglas-Hamilton farm. Many bush pilots flew in as well to offer support (far left).

Iain Douglas-Hamilton led the Vimy north with his Cessna 185, across the Great Rift Valley to Samburu National Park, creating stunning photo platforms for the *Silver Queen* above the Ewaso Ng'iro River.

FAR LEFT: On the flight from Samburu National Park, the Vimy reached 13,000 feet for views of Mt. Kenya. The summit is another 4,000 feet higher.

COUNTERCLOCKWISE FROM LEFT: On the dirt runway at Samburu, the Vimy drew attention from Kenya Wildlife Service patrollers and a band of Samburu warriors, who performed an impromptu dance. A rainstorm passed through, considered auspicious by the Samburu, prompting even more dancing.

The Vimy banked a turn over
a herd of elephants in the
Masai Mara game reserve.

After descending from
Mt. Kenya, the Vimy passed
over the Ewaso Ng'iro River.

Herds of elephants and
wildebeests were migrating
in the Masai Mara.

After the *Silver Queen* landed on Richard Bonham's grass strip in the Chyulu Hills, a group of Masai, who own the land, greeted the crew and the plane with guarded curiosity.

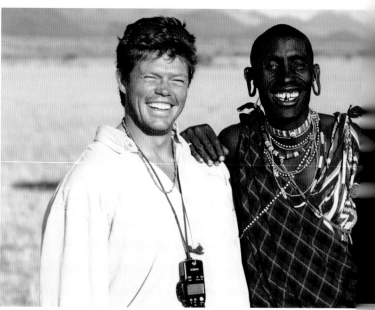

OPPOSITE, COUNTERCLOCKWISE FROM TOP LEFT: At the Chyulu Hills, the *Silver Queen* was parked in the shadow of Mt. Kilimanjaro. The Masai became increasingly intrigued by the Vimy when they learned of her fabric covering. They warmed up to the visitors, and one used Peter's camera for a shot of the photographer and a friend. A Masai warrior showed his annoyance after he allowed John to throw his spear, and it was returned bent.

LEFT: On July 19, the Vimy labored skyward to 13,000 feet for views of Mt. Kilimanjaro's snow-capped peak.

FAR RIGHT: A crosswind caught the *Silver Queen*'s 68-foot wings as the aircraft returned from Mt. Kilimanjaro. Despite both pilots' quick response, the starboard wing hit the dirt runway.

TOP LEFT: After recovering the landing, the team inspected the damage. The bent aileron control wasn't severe but would require time and parts for repair.

ABOVE LEFT: Frustrated that he was running out of leave time from his job, Mark decided to return to Nairobi and look for better fuel caches in Tanzania.

TOP: After leaving Peter to watch the plane, John went to Nairobi in search of parts.

ABOVE: Using limited tools, John straightened and tightened the aileron control.

Hopping their way through central Tanzania, the team stopped in Dodoma for fuel and then landed in Mbeya.

TOP: After the *Silver Queen* arrived unannounced in Mbeya, Tanzania, a crowd started to form around the plane as John asked where to find fuel.

ABOVE: Within minutes, thousands encircled the plane, laughing and hollering.

RIGHT: Although at first concerned about the amassing crowd, the team soon realized that the majority of spectators were giddy children eager to see why the giant "flying kite" came to their town.

After climbing through dense clouds in southern Tanzania, the Vimy was forced over the Malawi Mountains before reaching open, blue skies over Lake Malawi. Following a night in Malawi and a stop in Zambia, the team lumbered into Livingstone International Airport on a clear morning as the Zambian Air Force practiced marching skills on the tarmac. The curious soldiers surrounded the Vimy, and one stated, "When I saw you in the sky, I wondered what kind of time machine you were." The following day, the team was rewarded with a view of the Zambezi River and the earth-splitting Victoria Falls during a photo flight with support from a local helicopter company. Mist rose above the falls, which locals refer to as "smoke that thunders," and the Vimy passed near the rising cloud and its accompanying rainbow before pushing on to Zimbabwe.

First Aerial Image

The first aerial photograph of Victoria Falls taken by Sir Quintin Brand, from the Silver Queen, March 1920.

On a clear, blue-sky afternoon on July 24, 1999, the *Silver Queen* departed from Livingstone, Zambia, and slowly climbed to 1,000 feet. Turning southeast, the crew headed toward Bulawayo, Zimbabwe. Below, the Zambezi River, forming the border between Zambia and Zimbabwe, wound its way through the flat savannah and then suddenly dropped into a chasm, creating Victoria Falls. As the Vimy flew over the mist or "smoke that thunders" that builds over the raging waterfall, the crew crossed almost exactly the dusty trail of their predecessors. In 1920 Quintin Brand took the first aerial photograph of Victoria Falls, showing its power and beauty from the sky. Seventy-nine years later, having studied Brand's photo closely, we purposefully flew the same route in order to capture the same image, and compare then and now. In both photographs, a cloth-covered Vimy wing frames the falls. For a split second, despite the intervening decades, John, Mark, and I felt as if we were touching the past—flying in a distant time over an older Africa.

Bulawayo, Then and Now

On the evening of July 24, 1999, the *Silver Queen* replica touched down at Bulawayo International Airport to cheering crowds and marching bands. Some of the well-wishers had witnessed the *Silver Queen* landing on March 5, 1920. It was the first aircraft they had ever seen. To watch another *Silver Queen* float from the sky brought tears to the eyes of many. The original pilots, Pierre van Ryneveld and Quintin Brand, buoyed by the cheering crowds, capped off their tanks and took off promptly for Pretoria, South Africa. The overloaded plane was unable to gain altitude and crashed a mile outside Bulawayo. None of the four-member crew or the cat on board was injured, but the airframe was destroyed. Today, a humble, often unnoted stone monument sits on the site. Eager to complete the race, the two South African pilots flew the remaining leg to Cape Town in the *Voortrekker*, a single-engine D.H.9. They were met with great fanfare but failed to win the *Daily Mail* prize since they did not complete the journey in their original Vimy. The South African government later awarded each pilot £5,000.

ABOVE AND TOP RIGHT: Locals surrounded the *Silver Queen* when it landed in Bulawayo, and marching bands celebrated the crew's arrival.

FAR LEFT: Two women teared up as they awaited the arrival of the replica *Silver Queen*. In 1920, the Vimy was the first airplane they ever saw when it first reached what was then Southern Rhodesia.

LEFT: Mark and John were presented with gifts, including miniature Vimy replicas.

RIGHT: Despite the festive receptions, including a banquet dinner at the Bulawayo Club, the *Silver Queen* was far from its goal. More than 16 hours of flying over desolate country remained before the crew would reach the bottom of the continent.

Much of Africa had changed between 1920 and 1999, but the aerial perspective revealed unaltered patterns such as this village in Zimbabwe.

Over Mozambique, the crew had
a view of game and livestock trails
crossing a farm road, a sight that
van Ryneveld and Brand likely had
witnessed decades earlier.

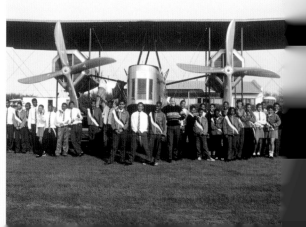

Educational Ambassadors

In July 1999 five students from five different countries gathered in a cheap hotel room in Nairobi, Kenya, to begin a unique educational adventure traveling alongside the remade *Silver Queen* airplane. The students, who ranged from 14 to 18 years of age, along with Matt Bresler and me, passed the first couple weeks in tense anticipation. We kept busy with various cultural projects and by visiting local schools and experiencing the landscape and wildlife of north and central Kenya. Uncertain political circumstances left us unsure whether we'd be going home without ever rejoining our mates or the plane. Finally, various winds shifted, and we were able to connect with our friends and the beautiful airborne relic on an airfield in Nairobi. The students jumped right in to help maintain the plane and participate in the final legs of the journey.

On our way to Cape Town, we brought a geographical context to the project by studying African cultures and history and tracking rare wildlife. We even crept up under a leopard in a tree with his lunch, a 300-pound antelope. We watched lions mating, ran from thundering elephants, and dove under our van to avoid a swarm of giant African bees. With poise beyond their years, the team lectured at local schools and spoke to the media, describing the project, the plane itself, and their own lifestyles and cultures to masses of children young and old. With two old laptops and some ingenuity, we also put all the adventures together in words and photos for the still-infant World Wide Web.

For me, the most dramatic and touching cultural experiences were played out among the students as they explored the harmonies and conflicts of their own backgrounds and personalities in some of the toughest and most demanding settings and circumstances possible.
—Mick Follari

LEFT: The *Silver Queen* finally reached Cape Town and soared below Table Mountain.

TOP LEFT AND RIGHT: On the way to Cape Town, the *Silver Queen* fought winter weather, including thick cloud cover, rain, and even snow, giving Mark added concern about the team's flying time.

ABOVE LEFT: On July 29, the plane touched down at Cape Town International Airport to a gathering of press and well-wishers, including Anthony van Ryneveld, a relative of Pierre's.

ABOVE: Wearing the same clothes they had when they departed England, Mark, John, and Peter celebrated their arrival on the shores of the Cape, holding the daily paper with the Vimy on the cover.

Before dismantling the aircraft to ship it to California, Lang Kidby and John LaNoue toured the shores of Cape Town, showing off the flying museum to small towns around the Cape.

{ 2001–2005 }

Touring
North America

*To Remind and
Inspire*

The Vimy Comes Home

by Peter McMillan All the bits and pieces that make up the Vimy returned to California from South Africa in December of 1999. John LaNoue set up shop in a hangar at the Marin County Airport, a short distance up the road from where she had been constructed six years earlier. Once again out of money, we had to rely heavily on our key volunteers, Ed Bullian and Bill Totten, as well as on John's good graces in between his jobs constructing sets for feature films. Our Vimy had weathered through harsh conditions on her journeys to Australia and Africa. Some of the fabric was sagging and tattered, and in need of replacement after the wind had beaten on it for more than 400 hours. Then there were the holes from my dropping tools and spark plugs through the lower wing.

Time to Show Off

On our full shakedown roundtrip cruise up to Seattle and back, we logged about 26 hours and had a spectacular view of Mt. Rainier as we approached Boeing Field. I circled the Space Needle at a range close enough to see the astonished looks of those against the observation railing. We had a few glorious days flying around Friday Harbor and Orcas Island, Washington, where David Holbrooke had arranged for students in the local schools to touch the aircraft and hear of our adventures in Europe, Asia, and Africa.

Back in the Bay Area, we flew in a few air shows, and upon return from one such event in Half Moon Bay, as we rolled out on landing, the right gearbox sounded like a blender full of rocks, the result of a multiple bearing failure. We had been extremely fortunate that the massive gears had retained enough of their integrity to keep the prop turning as we crossed over the Golden Gate Bridge and San Francisco Bay.

Replacing the damaged gears turned out to be a nine-month ordeal, and once again our resources and determination were put to the test, but in April of 2001 the Vimy was finally ready. Our first event was a fly-over display as part of the grand reopening of Crissy Field in the San Francisco Presidio, near the south end of the Golden Gate Bridge.

In July 2001 we managed to fly her from California to the EAA AirVenture in Oshkosh, Wisconsin, the world's largest aviation event. Flying duties were shared among a group of us. We drew crowds at all our whistle stops in Arizona, New Mexico, Nebraska, Kansas, and Iowa, which reminded us of our 1994 tour across Australia. On arrival in Oshkosh, the Vimy was given the place of honor among the 15,000 planes attending the show. When we rolled her out to fly, we marveled at the perfect outline of the

NORTH AMERICAN FLY-ABOUT: Approximately 11,000 miles

PILOTS: Dan Downs, Gary Isaacs, Gary Kent, Will Klein, John LaNoue, Peter McMillan, Shawn Mulligan, Mark Rebholz, Tina Ziolkowski

Peter McMillan and Gary Isaacs
pried themselves out of the cockpit
after the flight from San Francisco
to Friday Harbor, Washington.

Vimy that remained in the grass—a tribute to the tens of thousands of well-wishers who had stood to have a close look at our well-traveled machine. Total flying time to Oshkosh and back to California was more than 90 hours due to steering around the highest of the Rocky Mountains and the midwestern thunderstorms. Nevertheless, attending this mecca for aviation enthusiasts was worth the effort.

New Engines and New Partners

Over the course of 2002 and 2003, we held many meetings among the various team members to discuss the logistics and expenses of re-creating the 1919 Atlantic crossing by John Alcock and Arthur Whitten Brown. At these gatherings we would look each other in the eyes to see if we really had the energy for one last adventure, even though we didn't have the money. In the past, the determination had always led us to the resources.

The gearbox problems were a concern, and our experience on the flight to South Africa indicated that our BMW engines might not be adequate to lift the extra fuel required. We estimated a need for a range of 22 hours, or as much as 7,000 pounds of fuel. Over the next year, we gathered finances, and in 2004 struck a deal with Orenda Recip Engines of Toronto for new engines, thanks to the adventurism of Ken Smythe and Derek Parker. John LaNoue girded for battle now that he had to pull off yet another engine change—this one by far the most complex. A bonus of the Orenda deal was that it brought along an invaluable resource in Sebastien Arsenault, who came down from Canada to support John with the installation, which involved building entirely new oil, exhaust, and electrical systems. Seb was no stranger to harsh conditions, having serviced de Havilland Otters in northern Quebec. Spending night after night in the hangar was not a particular hardship.

Costs were escalating, and we had tapped most of our sponsors and donors. As seemed to happen so frequently throughout the Vimy project, we needed a minor miracle. I became acquainted with an agent from Steve Fossett's worldwide adventure organization who indicated to me that Steve might be interested in taking the helm across the Atlantic. Fresh from his spectacular success flying the Virgin Global Flyer around

ABOVE: The crew looked down on San Juan Island, Washington. At Friday Harbor, they gave rides to many locals.

RIGHT: The Vimy buzzed low over a cruise ship passing through Puget Sound. Those on deck seemed to enjoy the late-afternoon air show.

FAR RIGHT: A 1930s Waco biplane formed up alongside the Vimy at sunset, with the archipelago near Orcas Island, Washington, visible in the background.

TOP: The skyline of downtown San Francisco was the backdrop as the Vimy orbited the bay.

ABOVE: The Vimy was part of the air show on May 6, 2001, that celebrated the reopening of Crissy Field at San Francisco's Presidio. She cruised above Fisherman's Wharf.

RIGHT: Finishing her air show routine, the flying machine retreated from San Francisco Bay and headed north over the Golden Gate Bridge.

the world without stopping or refueling (or sleeping very much), Steve was keen to try a low-level, all-manual adventure. He was the perfect partner: his broad experience was useful, and his will and stamina would prove critical. Sadly, this meant that I had to give up the pilot seat.

There was one more complication. Mark was steadfast that he would conduct the navigator's duties exactly as Arthur Whitten Brown had—using compass and sextant only, no GPS or navigation radios. This feat would require that he obtain the dodo bird of airman ratings. He would need to become a card-carrying Flight Navigator, or the Canadian authorities would not let the Vimy advance a single mile toward Ireland.

The testing phase in the winter of 2004–05 was tedious and tiring. John would work all day, and I would join him at the hangar in Marin County around 8 p.m. on most nights. The two of us would wrestle the huge biplane outside and run the engines night after night. Air testing commenced in March, and we delivered the Vimy to Sanders Aircraft near Sacramento, where the new fuel system was installed.

Another Step Closer to Ireland

Mark and Steve started familiarization flights, and in May set off on the 4,000-mile journey to St. John's, Newfoundland. Quite a few problems were shaken out along the way. John and Sebastien rejoined the aircraft in Toronto for a week of festivities. We had another grand reception from the staff of the Canada Aviation and Space Museum in Ottawa. John and Mark took the spectacular legs up the St. Lawrence Seaway and then across Atlantic Canada to Newfoundland. On June 9 the Vimy finally arrived in St. John's, after 12 years of preparation.

Once again, it was time to wait for a while. Steve Fossett rejoined the team in St. John's, and the air was charged as the Vimy was made ready for departure on June 14, the anniversary of the 1919 flight, but a failed voltage regulator popped the swelling balloon of excitement. Two more weeks of bad weather ensued. Time was running out for Mark and Steve and for the rest of the crew, all of whom had other obligations.

The first few days of July showed a high pressure system above Bermuda and low pressure in the North Atlantic—the combination that would produce the pinwheels creating strong tailwinds needed along the flight path. However, cloud cover, the other critical weather factor, was uncertain. Some visibility would be essential for navigating safely. Mark and Steve made the call—it was on to Ireland.

FAR LEFT: Mark Rebholz demonstrated the motions of Arthur Whitten Brown, navigator on the 1919 transatlantic flight, who had to rise out of the cockpit and clear the fuel flow gauge of ice. Gary Isaacs was the pilot for this flight.

ABOVE: The ancient-looking Vickers bomber taxied in front of a C-17 transport plane at Oshkosh, Wisconsin.

LEFT: A perfect silhouette shows the lattice work of bracing wires that make up the prodigious strength of the Vimy's airframe.

ENGLAND-AUSTRALIA-11,234 MI
NOVEMBER 12 - DECEMBER 10, 1919
SEPTEMBER 11 - OCTOBER 22, 1994

NATIONAL
GEOGRAPHIC
SOCIETY

ENGLAND   FRANCE   ITALY   GREECE   EGYPT   SAUDI ARABIA

PAKISTAN   INDIA   BURMA   SINGAPORE   INDONESIA

OPPOSITE: The right side of the aircraft showed the countries and mileage covered on the journey from England to Australia. The flag of Thailand was removed to make a hole for the drift meter that the crew would need for dead reckoning their way across the Atlantic.

LEFT: There was always another task to complete. From stem to stern and even underneath, the mammoth biplane was in need of constant attention, in this case trueing up the undercarriage and checking the bracing wires.

BELOW: Steve Fossett's personal kit for the transatlantic flight.

Switching Engines

The conversion to the Orenda OE600 engines began in earnest in 2002 and took the better part of two years. It also confronted us with the proverbial conundrum of trying to squeeze 10 pounds of stuff into a 2-pound sack. In comparison to our previous installations, the Orenda engines demanded a considerably greater amount of additional accessories in order to operate. All this equipment had to be integrated into a design layout that would not only conform to the shape of the original cowlings but also provide for an efficient, ergonomic use of space and ease of maintenance.

Proper engine cooling is always at the top of the priority list when designing a new engine installation. Our experience with the two previous engine packages taught us many valuable lessons. The Orenda engines, with their greater horsepower, demanded larger radiators as well as an efficient air-ducting system to support them. Additionally, the Orendas were equipped with large turbo-chargers that required an intercooler to chill the compressed air prior to its entry into the engines' induction system. These intercoolers were not much smaller than the radiators used in our V12 package and required their own complex air ducting. —John LaNoue

TOP LEFT: Flying was always best just after sunrise. The primitive machine would struggle during the hottest parts of the day, particularly if carrying a heavy fuel load.

TOP RIGHT: The Vimy, newly fitted with Orenda engines, was tested over Northern California.

ABOVE LEFT: Mark Rebholz and John LaNoue flew the Vimy across Arizona on the journey to Wisconsin in 2001.

ABOVE: In July 2001, the crew flew the Vimy from San Francisco to Oshkosh, Wisconsin, for the annual EAA AirVenture event, passing over Lake Michigan.

LEFT: Steve Fossett and Mark Rebholz (right) answered questions about their upcoming transatlantic flight before the Vimy departed Salina, Kansas.

ABOVE: Steve stood proudly in front of the Vimy before a test hop.

RIGHT: En route to Newfoundland, in Salina, Kansas, the Vimy parked next to the Global Flyer, which Steve had flown solo, nonstop, around the world in March 2005.

In the late spring of 2005, the excitement built during the Vimy's flight across the United States and Canada. Crowds and the press became ever present as she came closer to St. John's, Newfoundland, the start of her final great adventure. Mark Rebholz and John LaNoue (right) and Steve Fossett (far left center) patiently answered questions day after day. The most common query was "Why are you doing this?" The pilots surely wondered the same.

The Vimy rested in Toronto the evening before Mark Rebholz and John LaNoue started for Newfoundland. Unfortunately, the weather was not so benign as the Vimy flew east and north through Ottawa and Atlantic Canada.

England–South Africa–9,082 Miles
February 1–March 20, 1920
June 3–July 29, 1999

NATIONAL GEOGRAPHIC

BAILEY & PARTNERS

John LaNoue
Builder

Bill Whitney
Designer

Wayne Daley
Fabricator

Dan Nelson
Fabricator

David Holbrooke
Fueler

LEFT AND ABOVE: The Vimy reached Toronto on May 25, 2005. The new Orenda engines had performed well on this shakedown mission from California. For several days, the crew and the Orenda team thoroughly inspected the engines before the Vimy headed to Newfoundland.

RIGHT: In Toronto, a group of World War I fighter replicas joined the Vimy.

ABOVE: All the bolts and nuts were secured in a final inspection before the Vimy ventured almost 2,000 miles across the frigid North Atlantic. The pilots got most of the glory, but the careful eyes and hands of the engineers ensured that the machine stayed in the air for nearly 20 straight hours.

RIGHT: Wires, laces, hoses, cables, struts, and bolts—all come together to form, as Ross Smith said, "the nearest thing to animate life that man has created." At top right is the original control wheel from 1919.

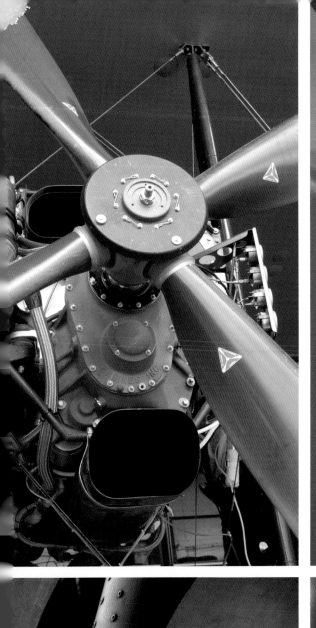

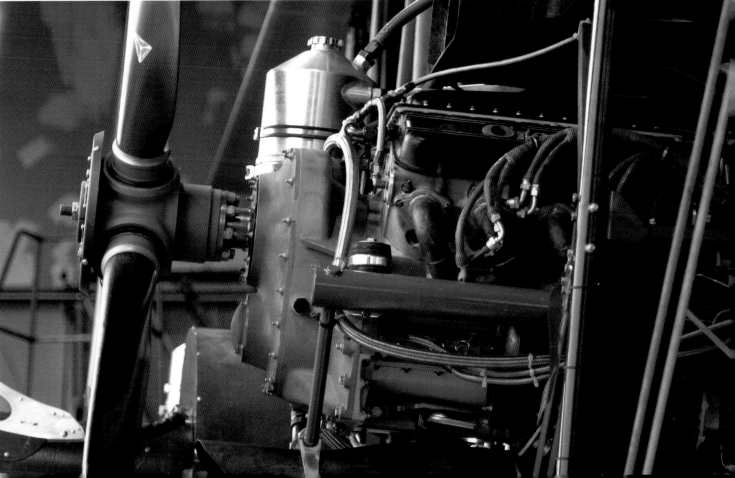

Into a foreboding twilight, the Vimy headed out over the water. Mark Rebholz recalled, "Even after years of preparation, when the last green strip of Canada slipped below the horizon behind us, I had to take a breath and contemplate the awesome amount of ocean before us."

{ 1919 | 2005 }

Crossing the Atlantic

"Yesterday I was in America"

The Vimy departed Lester's Field outside St. John's. One of the numerous delays was caused by a broken bungee cord. The cords served as shock absorbers for the undercarriage. The ground crew had to remove all 865 gallons of fuel with a small hand pump, jack up the wheels, and remove the bungees. The process took six hours of backbreaking labor.

The Atlantic Challenge

by Peter McMillan In the spring of 1919, England remained in a state of numbness from the horrors of World War I. As people slowly began picking up the pieces of their shattered lives, they needed something to give them courage, to inspire them. Into this breach stepped Lord Northcliffe, founder of the *Daily Mail,* who offered a prize equivalent today to $1 million to the first aviators to fly nonstop between North America and England.

Rolls-Royce joined forces with aircraft maker Vickers to enter a Vickers F.B.27 Vimy biplane in the contest, shipping the giant aircraft in pieces to Newfoundland, Canada. All other entrants had to do the same, as only with the help of the prevailing winds from west to east would it be possible to make the nonstop 2,000-mile voyage. Commanding the Vimy was one of the most experienced airmen in England, Captain John Alcock. Jack, as he was commonly known, had been a pilot since 1912. He had survived hazardous action in the war while flying night bombing missions against the Turks, ultimately sitting out the last year of the war in a prison after a splintered prop forced him down in waters near the Macedonian coast.

Solving the problem of weight (fuel) versus range versus speed versus pilot endurance was one of Alcock's specialties. Still, the Atlantic flight offered a more daunting problem: navigation. Though sailors had been navigating the seas for thousands of years, aerial navigation was, in 1920, still a matter of reading map and compass. Mariners had perfected the art of fixing stars with a sextant by reference to the horizon. But how could the same be done in a vibrating machine that was moving at a hundred miles per hour? Arthur Whitten Brown made a study of possible solutions during his countless hours in captivity after he had been shot down by the Germans in 1916. Brown had approached Vickers for employment upon his repatriation and was appointed to the Atlantic team after articulating his theories on great circle navigation, drift computation, and using a level attached to a sextant to simulate marine conditions.

By April 1919, four teams were headed for Canada to compete for the *Daily Mail* prize. On arrival in St. John's in early May, the Vickers team of 13 set about finding a suitable field and then assembling the Vimy in very harsh and primitive conditions.

TOP LEFT: The Sopwith Atlantic flown by Harry Hawker incorporated a small lifeboat in the rear fuselage.

TOP RIGHT: John Alcock (left) and Arthur Whitten Brown were very different personalities, but they shared a number of experiences, including growing up in industrial Manchester.

ABOVE CENTER: Alcock and Brown carried a very basic compass on their flight and navigated using a sextant.

ABOVE: Alcock and Brown regularly checked the reassembly of the Vimy, which had been shipped in pieces from England.

TOP: Built at Brooklands especially for the transatlantic flight, the Vimy used by Alcock and Brown was reconstructed at Lester's Field by a team from Vickers.

ABOVE: The Vimy and other competing machines made St. John's a tourist attraction for all of Atlantic Canada. Few among the crowds in the remote region had ever seen an aircraft.

OPPOSITE: Alcock and Brown landed in a bog near Clifden, Ireland (bottom), shown in a famous image. Relieved after their successful crossing, they signed autographs for eager admirers (top).

The Sopwith Atlantic Takes Off

Suddenly, on May 18, Harry Hawker and his navigator, Robert Mackenzie-Grieve, departed in their custom-built single-engine biplane dubbed the *Sopwith Atlantic*. Among her unusual features were an undercarriage that was dropped after takeoff to reduce drag and a petite dinghy that was carried upside down in the rear fuselage. The little aircraft made it through the night without incident despite bouts with foul weather, but in the early morning hours, the radiator malfunctioned roughly halfway across the ocean. As the engine began to boil, Hawker alternately climbed, switched the engine off, and then dove to cool it again. Soon the situation became hopeless, and the engine seized.

It was no minor miracle when Hawker came down through the low mist to see a small steamship a few miles away. He fired flares to ensure that the vessel, the Danish ship *Mary*, had seen them. The 12-foot swells were challenging, but Hawker ditched successfully, and he and Mackenzie-Grieve quickly entered the dinghy. The slow freighter maneuvered to within 200 yards of the airmen. Given the wind and waves, it took nearly two hours to get them aboard the ship's launch and ultimately aboard the *Mary*. The ship lacked a radio, so there was no way to inform the anxious world that the men had been saved.

Concern grew first into fear and then despair. Only Hawker's wife, Muriel, stayed steadfast. She quickly became a national figure—a symbol of the courageous English woman. Lord Northcliffe offered her the *Daily Mail* prize money as a consolation for her loss. She thanked him but added, "I cannot and will not believe that my husband is not alive." On the sixth day, Saturday, May 24, she received an eloquent note of sadness and sympathy from King George V. The Sunday papers announced "all hope was lost." Muriel dismissed the news and went to church. When she returned, the phone rang: Hawker and Mackenzie-Grieve were alive.

All Britain erupted in a frenzy of celebration that lasted a week, fueled by the audacity of the event and by the character and celebrity of Muriel Hawker. Among the first telegrams to Muriel: "The King rejoices with you and the nation on the happy rescue of your gallant husband." There were parades, gigantic crowds, medals, prize money (Northcliffe gave the Hawkers £5,000), and tea at Buckingham Palace. The reportage was heady: "[More] than a sober addition to the science of flying—they have given a lesson in the art of living and dying...," wrote the *New York Globe*. "They have not only glorified a country, they have enriched mankind." All this was for a "failure." Others waited in Canada, braving the cruel spring.

Jack Alcock was said to have remarked, "Their hands will have blistered clapping for Harry Hawker...we'll be lucky to get a languid handshake should we get there!"

An Inauspicious Start

On the morning of June 14, 1919, the weather brightened enough that the Vimy team made preparations to get under way. Alcock and Brown packed snacks and a thermos of coffee. As mascots, they carried two stuffed toy black cats and a horseshoe that someone had nailed under the pilot's seat during the erection of the Vimy in St. John's. They also brought along a small bag with 197 letters, the first airmail from North America to Europe.

Heading into a 30-knot wind, Alcock coaxed the lumbering beast into the air at about 1:45 p.m. About an hour out over the roiling Atlantic, the small propeller that drove the generator was lost, rendering useless both the radio and the pilots' electrically heated flying suits. A few hours later, the left inner exhaust pipe cracked and flew away, which caused a continuous, deafening roar. Even more serious, the exhaust flame poured onto the bracing wires holding the wings, and soon the wires glowed red. Brown got a glimpse of the sun and then the stars from time to time, such that he was able to estimate their position.

Towering clouds ahead at 3 a.m. were impossible to climb over, and soon the Vimy was sheeted in ice. In a terrifying moment known only to those who have survived such episodes, the disoriented pilot lost control, and the Vimy spun down wildly. Ejected from the bottom of the cloud base, she was only a few hundred feet above the sea, upside down. Alcock had the presence of mind to push, rather than pull, on the control wheel. This leveled the aircraft, and only then did he roll her right side up.

Alcock climbed to 6,000 feet. Once again, the controls began to freeze, and the fuel flow gauges iced up. Myths surround what happened next, but Brown did not crawl on to the slippery wing. He kneeled on the fuselage and reached as high as he could to remove the ice. After several hours in and out of icing conditions, they were finally on top of the clouds at 11,000 feet but beginning to suffer from frostbite. Although morning light helped them see, the frozen ship was too difficult to control. Alcock brought the Vimy down through the clouds. The engines coughed, but the ice began to melt.

Ireland in Sight

The Vimy was now under full control, and the duo broke out of the clouds and saw the Atlantic. Within the hour, there were seabirds around, then at first a few rocky outcroppings and finally the green coast of Ireland. They crossed the coast flying over the Marconi radio station and considered pressing onward to England, but low clouds obscured the hills behind the village of Clifden. Alcock elected to land in what looked like a grassy meadow, but was a bog. The wheels splashed into the mud, and the Vimy pitched up, ingloriously breaking her nose as she burrowed into the ground. The sturdy machine, bruised but unbowed, had delivered her two airmen 1,900 unforgiving miles across the Atlantic Ocean.

Alcock and Brown, partially frozen, were elated as they stood up in the crinkled cockpit. Some young boys rushed up in amazement. Alcock tossed them an orange from his rations. "Have an orange from America," he cried. "I was there yesterday and I am the first man in Europe ever to say that!" The fliers were taken to a bed and breakfast where they cleaned up and were fed. Alcock's diary mentions that for the first day he felt hungry at "the wrong times"—the first person ever to describe "jet lag."

The news was wired to the *Daily Mail*. Despite Alcock's predictions that their feat would be eclipsed by the miracle of Harry Hawker, he and Brown were hailed as heroes. They emerged Sir John Alcock and Sir Arthur Whitten Brown, invested as knight commanders of the British Empire by King George V. Winston Churchill handed over the winner's purse at a grand luncheon at the Savoy Hotel. The race was over. Intercontinental air travel had just begun.

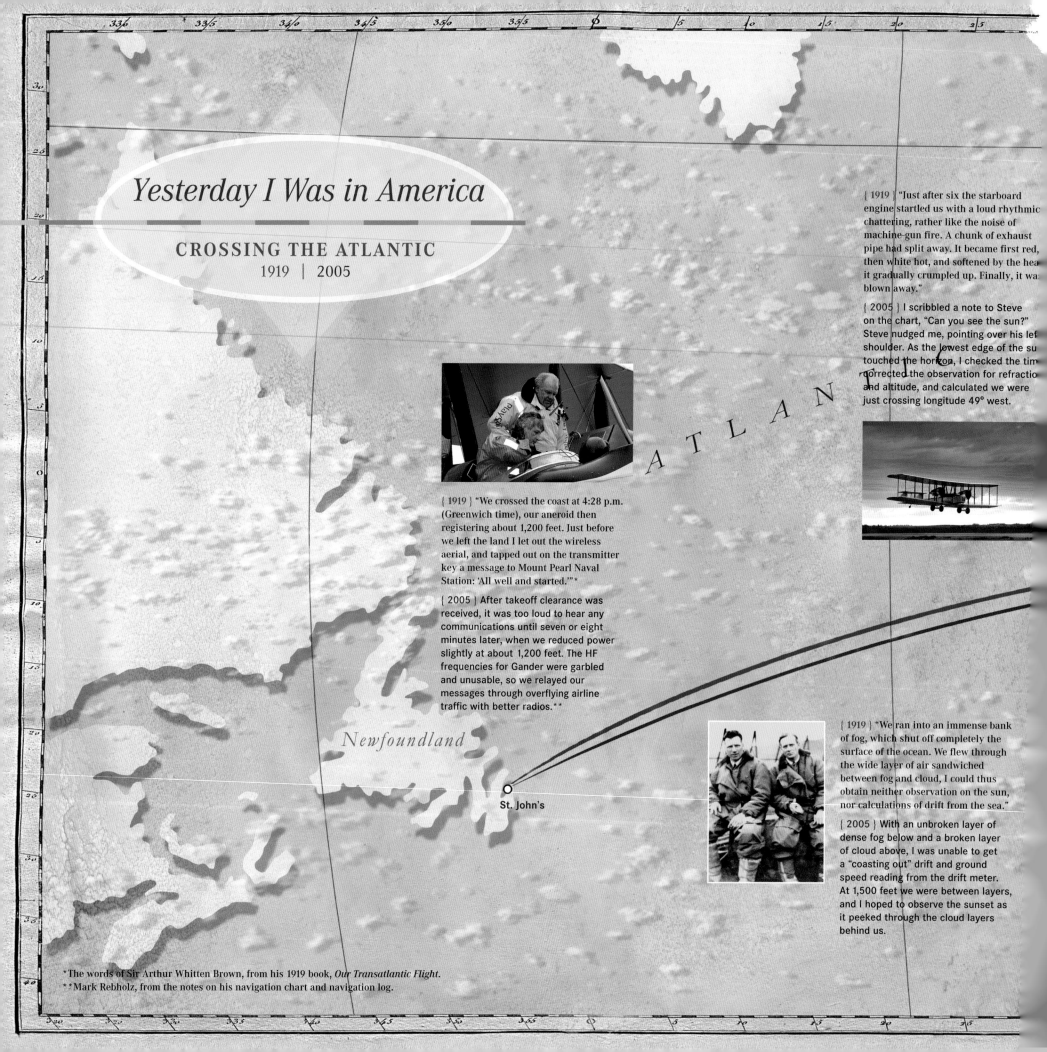

Yesterday I Was in America

CROSSING THE ATLANTIC
1919 | 2005

{ 1919 } "Just after six the starboard engine startled us with a loud rhythmic chattering, rather like the noise of machine-gun fire. A chunk of exhaust pipe had split away. It became first red, then white hot, and softened by the hea it gradually crumpled up. Finally, it wa blown away."

{ 2005 } I scribbled a note to Steve on the chart, "Can you see the sun?" Steve nudged me, pointing over his lef shoulder. As the lowest edge of the su touched the horizon, I checked the tim corrected the observation for refractio and altitude, and calculated we were just crossing longitude 49° west.

{ 1919 } "We crossed the coast at 4:28 p.m. (Greenwich time), our aneroid then registering about 1,200 feet. Just before we left the land I let out the wireless aerial, and tapped out on the transmitter key a message to Mount Pearl Naval Station: 'All well and started.'" *

{ 2005 } After takeoff clearance was received, it was too loud to hear any communications until seven or eight minutes later, when we reduced power slightly at about 1,200 feet. The HF frequencies for Gander were garbled and unusable, so we relayed our messages through overflying airline traffic with better radios.**

ATLAN

Newfoundland

St. John's

{ 1919 } "We ran into an immense bank of fog, which shut off completely the surface of the ocean. We flew through the wide layer of air sandwiched between fog and cloud, I could thus obtain neither observation on the sun, nor calculations of drift from the sea."

{ 2005 } With an unbroken layer of dense fog below and a broken layer of cloud above, I was unable to get a "coasting out" drift and ground speed reading from the drift meter. At 1,500 feet we were between layers, and I hoped to observe the sunset as it peeked through the cloud layers behind us.

*The words of Sir Arthur Whitten Brown, from his 1919 book, *Our Transatlantic Flight*.
**Mark Rebholz, from the notes on his navigation chart and navigation log.

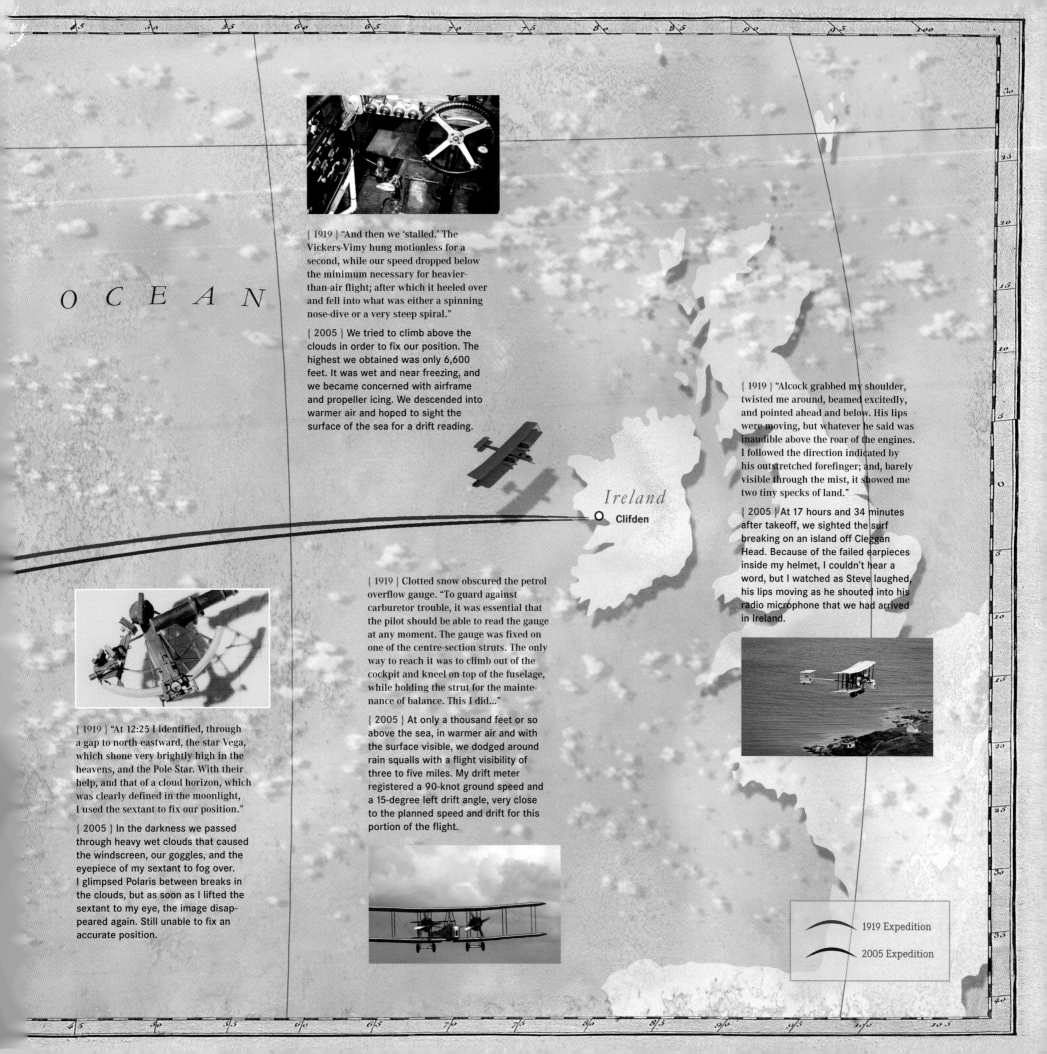

O C E A N

{ 1919 } "And then we 'stalled.' The Vickers-Vimy hung motionless for a second, while our speed dropped below the minimum necessary for heavier-than-air flight; after which it heeled over and fell into what was either a spinning nose-dive or a very steep spiral."

{ 2005 } We tried to climb above the clouds in order to fix our position. The highest we obtained was only 6,600 feet. It was wet and near freezing, and we became concerned with airframe and propeller icing. We descended into warmer air and hoped to sight the surface of the sea for a drift reading.

Ireland

○ Clifden

{ 1919 } "Alcock grabbed my shoulder, twisted me around, beamed excitedly, and pointed ahead and below. His lips were moving, but whatever he said was inaudible above the roar of the engines. I followed the direction indicated by his outstretched forefinger; and, barely visible through the mist, it showed me two tiny specks of land."

{ 2005 } At 17 hours and 34 minutes after takeoff, we sighted the surf breaking on an island off Cleggan Head. Because of the failed earpieces inside my helmet, I couldn't hear a word, but I watched as Steve laughed, his lips moving as he shouted into his radio microphone that we had arrived in Ireland.

{ 1919 } Clotted snow obscured the petrol overflow gauge. "To guard against carburetor trouble, it was essential that the pilot should be able to read the gauge at any moment. The gauge was fixed on one of the centre-section struts. The only way to reach it was to climb out of the cockpit and kneel on top of the fuselage, while holding the strut for the mainte-nance of balance. This I did..."

{ 2005 } At only a thousand feet or so above the sea, in warmer air and with the surface visible, we dodged around rain squalls with a flight visibility of three to five miles. My drift meter registered a 90-knot ground speed and a 15-degree left drift angle, very close to the planned speed and drift for this portion of the flight.

{ 1919 } "At 12:25 I identified, through a gap to north-eastward, the star Vega, which shone very brightly high in the heavens, and the Pole Star. With their help, and that of a cloud horizon, which was clearly defined in the moonlight, I used the sextant to fix our position."

{ 2005 } In the darkness we passed through heavy wet clouds that caused the windscreen, our goggles, and the eyepiece of my sextant to fog over. I glimpsed Polaris between breaks in the clouds, but as soon as I lifted the sextant to my eye, the image disap-peared again. Still unable to fix an accurate position.

⌒ 1919 Expedition

⌒ 2005 Expedition

John LaNoue checked the oil level on a bright day during the Vimy's extended stay in Newfoundland. One of the best weather windows for the Atlantic crossing was lost due to an electrical problem that required three critical days to source a new part.

The Atlantic Challenge, Reenacted

by Mark Rebholz In the years leading up to this moment, the beginning of the takeoff roll, I had tailored every bit of flight preparation so that I would not feel as I did then. But as I pushed the throttles forward and heaved the control column to fight the gusting wind, I felt rushed and ill prepared.

We had made the decision to launch only a few hours before, after many aborted attempts in better conditions, and I hoped that I had not compromised a little too much on the weather. My greatest concern was our need to minimize the time spent flying only by reference to our instruments. To do this, we would need to be above the clouds during the period of darkness so we could keep the wings level by the light of the moon. Our weather forecast showed clouds over the entire route, but clear above 5,000 feet at night. We slowly rose above the runway at St. John's only 90 minutes before sunset. The wind was howling, and as we passed Signal Hill on course for Ireland, our ground speed increased dramatically to over 100 knots.

Steve had a wide range of skills to draw upon, but nothing he had flown on his previous record flights was anything like this. Thankfully, he was a master of endurance and hardship, able to push himself through physical discomfort while conquering the given task. With the Vimy established in a stable but slow climb, I disengaged the control column and swung it over to his side, then reinstalled the locking pin to secure the wheel firmly in Steve's hands. I was finally free to do what I had been dreaming of for the past 12 years: navigating the Atlantic using traditional methods exactly as Arthur Whitten Brown did back in 1919.

We skimmed the tops of a fog layer as we crossed the Grand Banks. I was hoping to get a "coasting out" drift and ground speed reading from my vintage drift meter. But within minutes, we were between cloud layers with no sight of the waves only 1,500 feet below and several layers of broken clouds above. The engines were at the highest power setting, and we were barely staying on top of the clouds. When we occasionally slipped through a wet cloud, our windscreen and goggles instantly fogged over.

A Nonsmoking Flight

Even in the open cockpit of the Vimy with a 60-knot wind curling around the cramped interior, I could smell fuel. I anticipated a little fuel venting because we had experienced this in earlier test flights. I still needed to check it out. After unstrapping my harness, I turned around in my seat to

DEPARTURE: July 2, 2005; St. John's, Newfoundland, Canada

ARRIVAL: July 3, 2005; Clifden, Ireland

DURATION: 18 hours, 19 minutes, and 1,940 miles

PILOTS: Mark Rebholz and Steve Fossett

SUPPORT: Sebastien Arsenault, Patrick Joyce, John LaNoue, Jenny Moseley

kneel over the 200-gallon bladder tank immediately behind me. Droplets of fuel around the vent tube were blasting off toward the tail as the wind caught them. I was not worried. The venting would stop soon now that we had leveled off. I made a mental note of the clearly defined horizon behind us, with the sun centered between layers of cloud. It wouldn't be long before sunset.

When I turned around and slid my feet down to the cockpit floor, the heels of my rubber exposure-suit boots suddenly slipped out from under me, and I plopped down into the seat. Looking down at my feet, I saw a large pool of fuel, and more fuel pouring over my shins and onto the floor. Essential radio equipment, electronics, switches, and wiring were all dripping with fuel. My immediate concern was fire, and I restrained myself from moving anything electrical. I didn't even want to press the push-to-talk button on the intercom to alert Steve. The fuel was venting

from the 116-gallon bladder tank that sits in the forward cockpit. It had been filled to capacity prior to takeoff, and once we climbed, the fuel had expanded, with nowhere else to go but through the vented fuel cap and spill out and around the bladder.

I considered turning back, but the airplane was too heavy to land without damaging the landing gear and possibly crashing. The lack of a fuel dump system meant that it would be hours before we could make a safe landing. I reached across Steve's lap to a valve on the left sidewall and selected the nose tank "on." Then, awkwardly reaching to the floor under Steve's seat, I selected the main fuel valve "off." After 10 minutes, the fuel stopped dripping, and 10 minutes after that, I got the nerve to press the intercom switch and inform Steve of our near catastrophic problem. I spent the next hour burning a few minutes of fuel from each of the seven tanks so the problem wouldn't happen again.

The Vimy remained parked in St. John's, as Mark Rebholz and Steve Fossett waited for improved weather. In the end they had to make the best of imperfect conditions.

Where Are We Now?

Steve was flying a compass heading that I had computed prior to the flight based on forecast wind conditions. I needed to see the surface of the sea in order to get a drift reading, but it was dark and gloomy below, and the sun was about to set behind us. I strained to turn around in my seat to observe the setting sun, but in the confines of the cockpit, every time I squirmed around, I would disturb Steve. I wrote on the chart, "Can you see the sun?" Steve nodded affirmative. I then scribbled, "Let me know when it sets."

Moments later, Steve nudged me and motioned over his left shoulder. I glanced back and saw the lowest edge of the sun just touching the horizon. I corrected the observation and calculated that sunset for us was at 2323 UTC. Referring to a tabulated chart torn out of *The Air Almanac,* I determined we were just crossing longitude 49° west, and

our latitude was somewhat south of 49° north. I measured the distance off the chart and spun out a ground speed of 103 knots on my circular flight computer. This corresponded with the predicted ground speed. I was satisfied that the actual winds aloft were probably close to the forecast. I prepared the position report for transmission.

HF radios in anything other than commercial or military aircraft are notorious for being weak and unreliable. I was able to get a marginal HF check with Gander prior to takeoff, but now the radio was useless. I tuned up the VHF frequency that all aircraft monitor when over the Atlantic. Several airmen answered my call. From our very low altitude, I was unable to talk to ground stations on either coast, but we never lost contact with the passing high-altitude aircraft. We made more than 20 position reports on our journey, and every one was relayed through an airliner with better radios than we had.

As the sky grew darker, our visible horizon between the cloud layers began to disappear. Steve had to rely on the artificial horizon, a small gyro instrument that told us our attitude. Keeping the wings level in a Vimy on a clear day is challenging, and at night, staring at a three-inch-diameter instrument, it was difficult. I had hoped to avoid this by flying on top of the clouds in moonlight. We were only about 2,000 feet high, and we did not have the performance to climb higher until we burned off more fuel. The only other gyro instrument was a turn needle that showed if we were in a left or right turn. If the artificial horizon instrument should fail, our lives would depend on Steve's ability to maintain control of the airplane. The Vimy has no trim controls, and it flies as if it has neutral stability.

As the Vimy swayed back and forth in the lively air, the artificial horizon gently rolled back and forth, the turn needle wobbled to and fro, and the magnetic compass gently swung through an arc of 30 degrees. This was not precision flying. I was nervous and concerned. The least bit of inattention could cause the Vimy to exceed a bank angle we could not recover from, especially in instrument conditions. With my hands on the engine controls, I kept an instrument cross-check going as if I was the pilot flying. In the faint red glow of the instrument lights, I saw Steve's lined face in stern concentration as he willed the Vimy to maintain heading. I was exhausted keeping up my cross-check, but Steve was working even harder to manipulate the heavy flight controls.

I then became concerned about our drift. I knew our longitude within a few miles. What I needed was our latitude to tell us if we were drifting left or right of course. A few breaks in the clouds allowed me to see some stars. I took my sextant from the hook under the instrument panel and began to set it up for a Polaris latitude shot. Polaris, the North Star, would be almost directly off our left side and about 50 degrees above the horizon, roughly our latitude. I set 50 degrees on the arc of the sextant and retracted the shades so I could see a clear image in the darkness. In daylight, these few preparations are fast and simple, but with poor lighting and constant wind, they seemed to take forever. I peered through the eyepiece to adjust the background light for the bubble. This action that comes so naturally for me in normal circumstances seemed to be about the limit of my ability, and I hadn't even found the star yet. We were skimming the top of a cloud layer, and every time we flew through the wet cloud, the eyepiece of the sextant fogged over.

We slowly gained height and had a few breaks in the clouds, allowing me to identify stars. If we could only climb 1,500 feet more, we would be well clear. The airplane rocked as we entered the very wet cumulus-type clouds, and water vapor drifted through the floorboards and engulfed our space. The useless windscreen turned opaque, and if our goggles were down, we would be blinded by the foggy lenses and have to raise them up in order to see. Suddenly we popped out the side of a cloud into the brilliant night sky, with a quarter moon off the nose and Polaris on our left. I turned sideways and brought the sextant up to my eye. Just as I centered the image of Polaris in my field of view but before I could get an accurate reading on it, we entered another cloud. This frustrating process recurred several times over the next hour or so. If we could only climb above the clouds!

Again we popped out of the clouds. This time the image of the moon and stars was not quite so brilliant. A very high layer of cirrus-type clouds was emerging from the northeast. The stars were quickly disappearing,

Celestial Navigation

The concept of navigating by the sun, moon, planets, and stars — celestial navigation — goes back hundreds of years. Early mariners and astronomers were able to see that a single star, Polaris (also known as the North Star), remained in the same position in the sky even as other stars appeared to rotate around it, caused by the rotation of the Earth.

Furthermore, the angle of Polaris above the horizon corresponded with the observer's latitude. When the observer was at the North Pole, Polaris would be directly overhead, or 90° above the horizon (latitude 90° north). When the observer was standing on the equator, Polaris would lie on the horizon (0° latitude). Anywhere between the equator and the North Pole, a navigator could measure the angle of Polaris above the horizon and determine his latitude. The sextant is the optical instrument used to measure this angle.

The navigator needs only a clear view of the celestial body and a well-defined horizon. If darkness or haze obscures the horizon, a "bubble" horizon, or spirit level built into the optics of the sextant, can be used.

The understanding of celestial concepts has improved over the years. Possessing both an accurate timepiece and an almanac, the navigator can determine the exact position of any celestial body and its relative position to the Earth, such that a hypothetical observer could see the body 90° directly overhead. This geographical position is known as the subpoint. The navigator measures the angle of the body above the horizon with a sextant, which then determines his distance from the subpoint. Two or three observations can determine the navigator's position anywhere on Earth.

Following weeks of waiting for repairs and for good weather conditions, Mark and Steve finally prepared to depart. They lifted off shortly before sunset on July 2.

and the moon faded until we were once again in total darkness. I shined the beam of my flashlight into the night, and there was nothing to reflect back. We were not in clouds, but in total darkness. The dim red glow of the instrument lights and the cherry red exhaust pipes were all we could see. Soon Steve and I were totally occupied with the instrument flying, and the navigation was suffering. I still had no way to determine if we were left or right of course.

With much dismay, I pulled from my pocket a small GPS receiver, a very compact unit powered by two AAA batteries that could last only six hours. It was meant for hiking, and I am sure that the manufacturer never intended it to be used in the middle of the Atlantic, especially on an airplane. I placed the unit on the cockpit glare shield, the only usable space where it could pick up a signal. After three minutes, the GPS receiver acquired enough satellites for a fix. I jotted down our position in north latitude and west longitude on the chart. Feeling tremendously guilty for using this modern concession to pure navigation, I calculated a revised heading to return to our planned course. I measured our progress on the chart and planned the next position report. Now that I knew our actual track and ground speed, I was able to compute our actual in-flight winds. I rationalized that by performing the motions of plotting, measuring, and computing, I was using traditional means as well as I could. I also felt much better knowing that I had our unplanned drift under control. At the same time, I felt more respect than ever for the bravery of Arthur Whitten Brown and John Alcock. In 1919 they were truly flying into the unknown whereas I did not have the courage to fly blindly across the Atlantic without knowing where we would end up.

A Very, Very Dark Night

We fell into a comfortable yet tense routine. We had no discernible horizon with blackness above and blackness below. Steve was busy with his difficult instrument flying, his hands holding the wheel and his eyes constantly dancing around the instrument panel. With my left hand curled around the engine controls, I made constant adjustments to synchronize the propellers and increase the power if we descended or decrease the power if we accelerated. I constantly adjusted for the best fuel-air mixture for our power setting and altitude. At 6,600 feet, it became obvious that we would not be able to top the clouds, so we leveled off and adjusted the power for an economical cruise setting. As we burned fuel, I regularly asked Steve to let go of the controls to check the trim. If the nose went up, I burned fuel from an aft tank. If the nose went down, I burned fuel from the forward tank. It took only a second to determine the lateral trim. That was good, because in only a few more seconds the wings would bank in whatever direction they wanted with no warning, and Steve would have to grab the wheel and regain control. I kept passing our position reports to Gander through passing airliners overhead. I couldn't wait for the sunrise and visual flying conditions.

After an eternity in darkness, the atmosphere around us began to get light. The temperature was near freezing, and we occasionally flew through light rain. The huge propeller blades flung the droplets into the

As the sun touched the horizon, Mark took readings and determined the aircraft's position. Shortly thereafter, the Vimy entered the clouds.

After battling clouds for more than 14 hours, much of the time in darkness, the Vimy broke into a brilliant morning light about four-fifths of the way across the Atlantic. For the first time in about a thousand miles, Mark could establish their position.

cockpit. We were both getting cold and were afraid of ice forming on the Vimy, so we decided to descend. As we went through multiple layers of clouds, the sky above began to break up a bit. Our first sighting of the sun was well after sunrise at 0723 UTC through a small break in a layer above, 9 hours and 37 minutes after takeoff. At the base of the clouds, about 1,500 feet, we could finally see the surface of the sea. The temperature was a tolerable 50° Fahrenheit, and the visibility about three miles. We could deviate visually left and right of course to avoid the heaviest rain. Sometimes we were surrounded by rain, so we hunkered down and drove straight through it.

Feeling much safer now that we had a horizon, I could take time to look around. The sea was various shades of dark gray, and we were low enough that I could see the primary and secondary swells. Whitecaps and foam blew off the wave crests, indicating at least 25 knots of wind at the surface. Every 10 minutes or so, a shaft of brilliant sunlight beamed down through a break in the thick clouds, then suddenly extinguished as if turned off by a light switch.

Then I realized that I couldn't hear anything.

A Golden Silence

Ever since our takeoff, the radio was an almost constant barrage of conversation between ourselves and other aviators. Now there was silence. My headset and microphone were completely dead as if I had cut the communications cord with a knife. By passing handwritten notes, Steve and I confirmed that the communications on his side of the cockpit were normal. From this point until landing, Steve handled the communications while I navigated and managed the power and fuel. I wrote out position reports every 40 minutes and passed them to Steve for transmission. I was disappointed that I could no longer communicate, but I realized that this was exactly the way it was for Arthur Whitten Brown. I was living the flight as he and Alcock did, free to be alone with my thoughts.

In Ireland, the arrival celebration was on hold. As with all the Vimy expeditions, machine malfunctions or red tape caused unforeseen delays. This was a problem as well for those eagerly awaiting a chance to see the primitive flying machine.

Now that it was safe to look away from the flight instruments, I pulled out my drift meter, secured it to the bracket on the side of the cockpit, and took a series of observations. At 1125 UTC, I noted on my chart a 90-knot ground speed and a 15-degree left drift angle. I compared the readings with my flight plan for the same time and found that I had computed a 94-knot ground speed and 10 degrees of drift in this area. We had obviously crossed the weather front and were drifting back to the north. I gave Steve a corrected heading to fly.

At 1520 UTC, 17 hours and 34 minutes after takeoff, we sighted the surf breaking on the shore of an island. The very thin line of white was hard to distinguish from the mottled colors of the sea, sky, and shadows. Minutes later, we saw more surf breaking to the south of the island, on the point of the mainland called Cleggan Head. We steered toward the point, and at 1542 UTC we crossed the coast and we were over Ireland.

I looked at Steve, and we both smiled. With a gloved hand, he pressed the push-to-talk button, and I saw his mouth moving as he shouted into his microphone. Extremely happy in my deaf silence, I motioned to Steve that I could take the controls. Having previously surveyed the area, I knew exactly where to fly from this point on.

I located Clifden and circled the village a few hundred feet above the rooftops. I saw the faces of people in the town square looking up at us. After a few turns, we flew a few miles south to the Alcock and Brown memorial. The parking lot, easy to spot on top of a craggy hill, was full of cars, and many tourists waved and smiled as we circled. From the memorial, it was easy to see the original landing sight a few miles away on the Derrygimla Bog. I turned the Vimy east and circled the small mound marking where the nose of the original Vimy dug into the soft earth, abruptly ending the first nonstop Atlantic flight. Alone with my thoughts, I was choked up with emotion thinking about what we had just accomplished.

The golf course was easy to find. Every road was crowded with cars, and thousands of people surrounded the fairway we had chosen as our landing ground. A brisk quartering crosswind aided our landing, and we stopped nice and short with a third of the fairway remaining. By flying the Atlantic, England to Australia, and England to Cape Town, the Vimy replica had accomplished what no other airplane had done. Puffy white clouds streaked across the blue sky, and shadows raced over the deep green grass of Ireland, and I could imagine the smiling faces of Brown and Alcock, van Ryneveld and Brand, and the Smith brothers looking down with approval. Much of the world has changed since 1919, and even with so much change, it remains the same.

RIGHT AND CENTER, TOP TO BOTTOM: When the Vimy reached Ireland, Mark took the controls from Steve. They circled the village of Clifden before heading to their landing site.

FAR RIGHT: The Vimy looked almost modern as she passed over the ruins of Bunowen Castle.

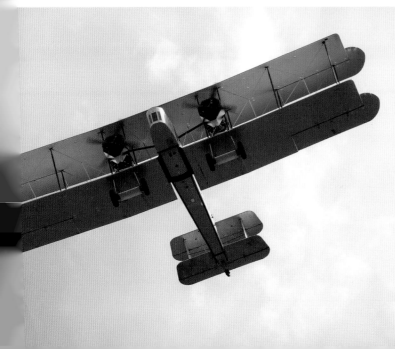

Casting a shadow on the bright green grass of Ireland, the Vimy crossed the boundary road for the Connemara Golf Links, the closest possible landing site to the bog where Alcock and Brown pitched up in the mud—less than a mile away from the course.

ABOVE, TOP TO BOTTOM: The Vimy's final touchdown in Ireland occurred at 12:18 local time.

RIGHT: Steve Fossett and Mark Rebholz were elated and relieved after overcoming numerous challenges in crossing 1,900 miles over the Atlantic Ocean in a primitive aircraft.

ABOVE: Minutes after the Vimy landed, the crowd that had been awaiting her arrival streamed onto the golf course to greet the crew and touch the plane. Later, when the celebrants dispersed, the golfers were allowed to resume play around the aircraft.

FAR LEFT: The crew quickly refreshed themselves with an Irish national treasure.

LEFT: Mark, Steve, and John enjoyed the victory parade in Clifden in a 1919 Rolls-Royce.

A swarm of well-wishers from Clifden and beyond greeted the pilots just after touchdown. It was probably a larger crowd than the one that welcomed Alcock and Brown in 1919, since their arrival was unexpected.

Epilogue

Touching the Past

While the Vimy was grounded by fog near Cairo, a young boy rushed up to the plane. The mammoth flying machine was a magnet for a new generation of adventurers at stops around the globe.

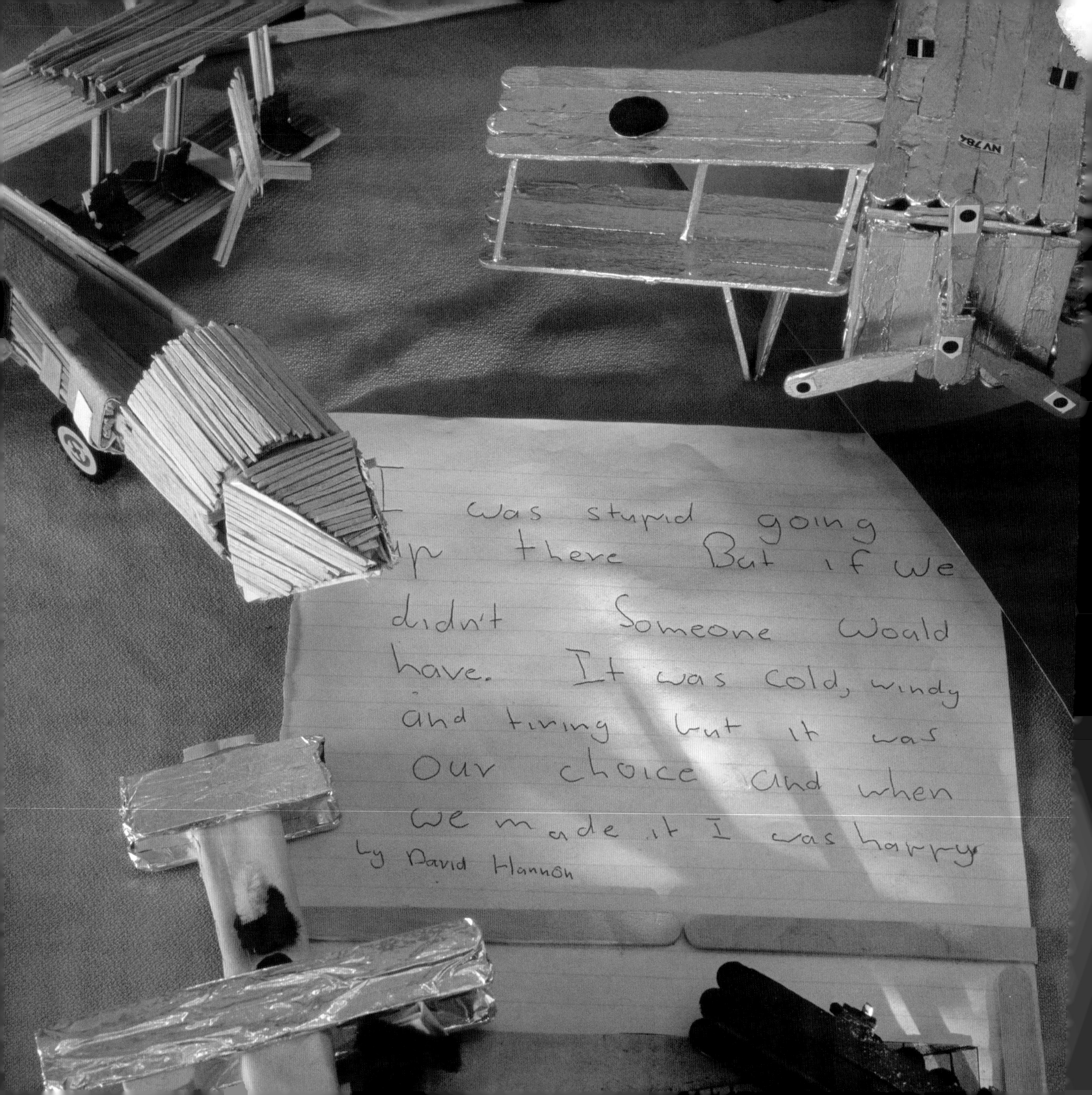

I was stupid going
up there But if we
didn't Someone Would
have. It was cold, windy
and tiring but it was
Our choice and when
we made it I was happy
by David Hannon

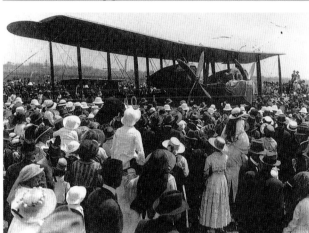

Adventure Never Ends

by Peter McMillan For all of us involved, seeing the Vimy in the morning sunbeams of Ireland on July 3, 2005, marked the summit of a long climb, more than a decade after Lang Kidby and I had first imagined what the consequences might be of restoring her to life. Like most adventures, ours had brought brief periods of glory at the cost of nearly continuous hardships and mishaps: damaged parts, broken promises, physical privation, financial trauma, false starts, encounters with opportunists, mountains of red tape and of fear. The ledger was hard to balance. On one side: careers left behind, 35,000 hours of construction, brushes with mortal danger, uncertainty of the outcome almost every day. On the other: the privilege of moving an unusual flying machine around the world at speeds slower than the average car on a motorway.

Few pioneering human endeavors, however, owe their origin to calculation. They arise from the human spirit. The quest for risk and for adventure, the desire to know what lies beyond the horizon—these imperatives are the lifeblood of human achievement. Our adventures involved a machine, but the motivating force lay deep within our hearts. We wanted to forge a kinship with heroes of the past, to see as they had seen and feel as they had felt, to revive not just their airplane but their spirit, in a world where we too often are discouraged from taking risks or from attempting dreams that others deem impossible.

Nor was our adventure over yet—not quite. Mark Rebholz and I retrieved the Vimy from the Connemara Golf Links and circled her above the town of Clifden in the steaming, early morning light. The weather soon turned appalling as we neared Shannon, forcing us to fly over the water at only 200 feet, beneath low clouds up the firth that would lead us to the airport. The cloud layer was lower than the height of the surrounding cliffs, and we were both stunned and alarmed to look up and see a cascading waterfall pouring just off the left wing.

We found our way to Shannon by a circuitous route that took an hour and a half to cover what would have been 47 direct miles. Mark, on unpaid leave from his job, needed to leave soon. John LaNoue met me in Shannon late that afternoon. With the weather improving slightly, we elected to push on 74 miles to Waterford to get fuel and be away early for our crossing of the Irish Sea to England. As Mark said farewell, he pulled me aside and advised, "I know the forecast seems adequate, but don't hesitate to land in a field if you are trapped by clouds."

The forward visibility was fair, about five miles, but when we were roughly halfway to Waterford, over County Tipperary, the ceiling squeezed us down to 300 feet. Although the many hills in the area were not particularly high, they were obscured and were certainly hard. John and I circled for about 30 minutes looking for a hole and then picked a large barley field with long grass for our landing at about 7 p.m.

OPPOSITE: Youngsters from the Australian outback town of Camooweal, Queensland, completed projects related to the Vimy, which served as a stimulus for learning about adventure and geography.

TOP, FROM LEFT: Miriam Alube, an 18-year-old from Kenya, winner of an essay contest, prepared to go aloft for her first ride. Gar Lasater (left) and John McBride (right) posed with Mark Rebholz. Kenyan students greeted the Vimy. The Vimy glided over Sydney Harbour.

ABOVE, FROM LEFT: *National Geographic* photographer Jim Stanfield always worked hard to get the perfect shot. Tessa Barroll, with Peter in Cairo, was the project manager handling logistics. Thousands came to see the first aircraft to fly all the way from England when the Vimy landed in Sydney on December 10, 1919.

Yet Another Unplanned Arrival

The touchdown was gentle, particularly compared to our jarring episode in Sumatra. On inspecting the Vimy, we discovered the only damage was a bent aileron horn under the left wing. Locals soon arrived offering all types of support (most had followed the Atlantic crossing), and within a few hours, the owner of the field showed up from his home in Cork. He was in a better bargaining position than were we, particularly since it was a bit too early to harvest. For a rather large sum, he agreed to cut part of the field and clear a runway the next morning. He then brought John and me down to the pub in the town of Cahir and treated us to a late steak dinner, confirming that he was pleased with the negotiation. As had happened so many times before, John and I met a wonderful group of people, sampled a taste of their daily life in an out-of-the-way corner of the world, and, within a few hours, were on a first-name basis with everyone in town. The Vimy continued to inspire that certain spirit of adventure and goodwill among all who saw her.

Once the hay was cut and baled, and the bales were rolled out of the path, we waved good-bye to the huge crowd from Tipperary, leaving clouds of barley behind as we departed. In our effort to minimize our financial damage, we had the field cut about 50 yards shorter than we probably should have. Our wheels swept tall grass immediately on liftoff.

The weather was better at Waterford, where we circled an international gathering of some 90 tall ships. We elected to brave the cold and climb to a height of 7,000 feet for our crossing of the Irish Sea. Once across the 100-mile ditch, John and I passed Strumble Head and were greeted by the spectacular geography in Wales—rugged shapes like the American West but carpeted in lush green. Upon our arrival at Turweston Aerodrome in central England, the controllers asked if we could make a flypast of the British Grand Prix, just a few miles away. We obliged and gave the crowd of half a million a good view of our well-traveled flying machine.

Lang Kidby, Mark Rebholz, John LaNoue, and I had other episodes that glorious summer of 2005, including landing on the front lawn at Woburn Abbey, the largest private home in England. But we knew that each flight brought us ever closer to the last. We would reflect in the air about one of the countless episodes we had endured or enjoyed—the hurricane in Pisa, the Taj Mahal, Victoria Falls—or we would recall some of the thousands of people who had helped us on our way or even saved the day. We noted the scars—a patch in the fabric where I had dropped a wrench back in Sumatra, a scrape on the wingtip from Kenya. I would look intently as the plane's large shadow scrolled across the earth. Each flight was bittersweet.

The end for many of our heroes had been bittersweet as well. Sir John Alcock died only six months after his Atlantic crossing in June of 1919, crashing in the fog of France while delivering a Vickers Viking amphibian to the first Paris Air Show after the war.

Arthur Whitten Brown, who had been Alcock's transatlantic navigator, shunned the fame of knighthood in favor of a sedate and bookish life in Manchester with his beloved wife, Kathleen. His tragedy came on June 6, 1944, when he lost his only son, who was serving as a fighter pilot above the beaches of Normandy. Four years later, Brown died of an overdose of medication. Most felt that he had taken his own life in despair.

What Is the Ultimate Price?

The most searing event occurred in April 1922. It was like old times as the Smith brothers, Sir Ross and Sir Keith, along with their tireless engineer, Jim Bennett, were swept up in a flurry at Brooklands as they prepared for the first circumnavigation of the globe. The three would fly the Vickers Viking, which could alight on land or water. A "press day" test flight was scheduled for late morning on Thursday, April 13. Keith was delayed returning from business in London, and though the newsmen were anxious, Ross elected to wait and share

The Spirits of the Past

In December 1919, G-EAOU was stranded on Ward Plain, a field outside Charleville, Queensland, due to an engine failure. After eight weeks of repairs, she was refueled (far left), and the crew continued on. Upon arrival in October 1994, Peter McMillan and Lang Kidby were informed by a local council member that the remote field was still vacant and reportedly contained some old fuel cans. The Vimy crew rushed to the scene to find the battered and rusty relics from the original flight. After enduring the hardships and doubts of their 12,000-mile journey, Peter said, "This was the first time that I felt we had been destined to make it." Lang, elated by the discovery, observed "that one man's junk is another man's treasure." The crew had touched the spirits of those long-lost pioneers of aviation.

the accolades with his older brother, whose steadiness had so many times buffered Ross's fearlessness. Eventually, the pressure prevailed. Ross turned and said, "C'mon Benny, let's giv'er a go." The high mounting of the Viking's rear-facing engine gave the machine some unusual handling characteristics. All went well until Ross cut the power for landing. Keith arrived just as the Viking entered a spin and smashed into trees near the Brooklands racetrack. Ross was dead by the time Keith had sprinted to the wreckage. Jim died in Keith's arms.

Ross Smith was fearless but not invincible; he had paid the ultimate price. He, like his Vimy brethren, knew that seeking new frontiers can be a dangerous and costly endeavor. But risk must not dissuade those fired to know more. It is the risk takers that build the long bridge from dreams to progress in any field. Ross Smith had a close friend, T. E. Lawrence, who said, "The dreamers of the day are dangerous men, for they may act their dream with open eyes, and make it possible."

We, the Vimy crew, hope our adventures have helped revive that spirit. Those who saw our magnificent flying machine, if only for a moment, say they felt a thrill and maybe a sense of optimism—the essential ingredient to getting any idea off the ground. The Vimy transported us not just through space but through time. The spirits of the past saw us repeatedly through the challenges and hazards of the present: 38 countries, miles and miles of earth and water, indescribable vistas, and thousands of lives touched.

Our unlikely flying galleon was a magnet for the next generation of explorers. Over 12 years we must have lifted more than 10,000 kids up onto the wing to have a closer look. It is a tactile machine; children could not resist drumming the fabric and thumping the wires. To them, it was sort of a dinosaur come to life. It had nothing in common with their concept of an aircraft. Kids would stare in amazement as they asked questions: "You flew this from where?" "Where do you go to the toilet?"

We conducted educational programs in dozens of cities and schools along the way in our effort to spread the spirit of pioneering. In advance of our arrival, teachers frequently had the students build models or write reports about the Vimy. One report in particular comes to mind, written by an eight-year-old, David Hannon from the tiny outback town of Camooweal, Australia. David wrote his report in the voice of Captain Ross Smith.

Name: Captain Ross Smith
Occupation: Hero

I was stupid going up there.
But if we didn't, someone would have.
It was cold, windy and tiring,
but it was our choice, and
when we made it, I was happy.

Let me tell you…we were happy too!

TOP: Jenny Moseley headed *National Geographic*'s operations in the UK and played critical roles in all three expeditions. David Holbrooke (right) envisioned and sponsored the project's educational activities.

ABOVE LEFT: Mick Follari, head of the student program for the Africa flight, lent a hand whenever he was needed.

ABOVE RIGHT: Kevin Weldon (left) and John Owen, of Weldon Owen Publishing, were intent that the Australian flight be documented in *The Greatest Flight* in 1995.

RIGHT: Mechanic Dan Nelson (above) contributed his formidable expertise to building the replica. One of the crew on the Australia flight, he helped repair the aircraft after the crash in Sumatra. Ed Bullian (bottom), a tireless volunteer throughout the Vimy's construction, strapped in for what would be his last flight after a career that spanned 60 years and many heroic episodes in World War II.

ONE FINAL MISADVENTURE

FAR RIGHT: After retrieving the Vimy from the golf course in Clifden, Peter and John attempted to make it to the east coast of Ireland but were trapped by low clouds and elected to land in a barley field in County Tipperary. Peter, standing in the cockpit, explained the circumstances to a bemused local.

LEFT: The Vimy made wavy tracks on landing in the ample barley field (top). Peter surveyed the improvised runway as the barley was baled and removed (bottom).

RIGHT: Peter and John bought a little bit of Ireland, as the field proved to be fairly expensive to prepare (top), but the local hospitality could not have been finer. John shared a bit of the Vimy saga with a local constable who came out to ensure that all was well (bottom).

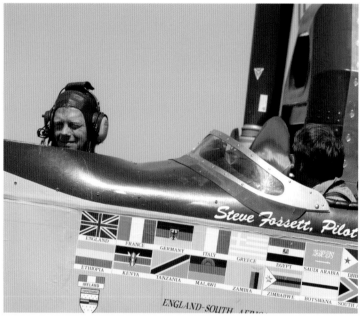

SCENES OF THE VIMY'S FAMILY

TOP ROW FROM LEFT: Sebastien Arsenault (right), Vimy engineer extraordinaire, with Peter McMillan at Woburn Abbey. The tail section is a repository of graffiti and stickers from around the world and a small memorial to Ed Bullian. The support crew in Toronto, Canada, made the final adjustments for the flight across the Atlantic.

MIDDLE ROW FROM LEFT: William Francklin, who hosted the Vimy crew, prepared for a flight. The McMillans picnicked at Woburn Abbey; Alston and Georgina sat on the wing, and Tessa held William. Peter McMillan (left) described the Vimy flights to an attendee at Turweston Aerodrome. Karin Owen, with her husband, David, hosted the Vimy at Turweston Aerodrome for the flypast of the British Grand Prix.

BOTTOM ROW FROM LEFT: HRH Prince Philip, an enthusiastic aviator, reviewed Peter's 1995 book *The Greatest Flight* during a ceremony at St. James's Palace. Brenda and John LaNoue were married in Clifden, Ireland; Mark Rebholz gave the vows, and Steve Fossett was best man. Admirers surround the Vimy on her tour of England.

LEFT: David Owen, owner of Turweston Aerodrome, surveyed the Vimy on her arrival.

LEFT: The Vimy zoomed over the English village of Wicken and the house of the Francklin family, who provided a hospitable retreat for the weary crew.

RIGHT: The mammoth biplane prepared to alight on the front lawn of Woburn Abbey, the ancestral home of the Dukes of Bedford and England's largest private house.

FAR RIGHT TOP: The Vimy circled above Woburn Abbey in preparation for landing at the annual Moth Rally held in August 2005.

FAR RIGHT BOTTOM: The Vimy banked over the village of Berwick in East Sussex.

The Evolution of the Vimy

by Philip Jarrett Famous as a "cradle of British aviation," Brooklands, in the county of Surrey, began in 1907 as the world's first purpose-designed motor-racing course, renowned for its steeply banked circuit. One or two aviation pioneers worked there briefly but unsuccessfully in 1907–08. Then, in late 1909, some of the land enclosed by the track was officially made available as an airfield. By April 1910 several amateur aviators were active on the site.

Brooklands soon attracted many solo experimenters and budding companies, which used it to test a wide assortment of flying machines. This hotbed of dedicated aviation pioneers became a thriving "Aviation Village" comprising several rows of wooden sheds. These innovators and risk takers shared their woes and triumphs, surviving on small incomes and basic but bearable communal meals at the famous Bluebird Cafe. Such renowned companies as Avro, Blériot, Deperdussin, Sopwith, and Martinsyde, some destined to be leading manufacturers in World War I, became established on the site, as did several flying schools.

Vickers Limited, one of the world's largest armaments manufacturers, began building aeroplanes in March 1911 at Erith in Kent. The company's first such product, the No. 1 Monoplane, made its maiden flight at Joyce Green, then was transported to Brooklands for further trials. Less than a year later, the Vickers Flying School was established at Brooklands. The school trained 77 pilots before the outbreak of war in 1914. One of them was Reginald ("Rex") Kirshaw Pierson, destined to become the Vimy's designer (opposite).

1915

With orders for aircraft on the rise following the start of World War I and its factories working at peak capacity, Vickers begins production at Brooklands. In less than two years, the factory is expanded twice.

1917

The first F.B.27, later named the Vimy, is flown in November. Rex Pierson, chief designer of Vickers Aircraft Division, oversees the F.B.27 design to meet a British Air Board specification for a heavy, multi-engine bomber.

1918–19

Following the Armistice of 1918, only 235 of the 1,000 Vickers Vimys ordered are produced. The first ones completed are flown to Egypt, where Royal Air Force squadrons employ them as bombers and transports.

1919

John Alcock and Arthur Whitten Brown fly a Brooklands-built Vimy nonstop from Canada to Ireland. After their achievement, Vickers designs a Vimy for commercial use. It seats nine passengers in open cockpits but is never built.

1919

Vickers produces its first aircraft designed to carry passengers in an enclosed cabin. The Vimy Commercial has its inaugural flight in April. The company provides a Vimy bomber for Ross and Keith Smith's flight from England to Australia.

The first Vickers twin-engine aeroplane was the E.F.B.7 fighter of 1915. The pilot was positioned behind the wings, and the gunner in the nose with a one-pounder Vickers automatic gun.

Rex Pierson's Life at Vickers

Rex Pierson (center), Sir Ross Smith (left), and Jim Bennett pose with the Vickers Viking amphibian shortly before the tragic flight that killed Smith and Bennett.

When Reginald Kirshaw Pierson was named chief designer of the Vickers Aircraft Division in 1917, he was put in charge of the company's design office in Knightsbridge, London. At the time of his appointment, he was only 26 years old.

Rex Pierson began his affiliation with Vickers in 1908, at age 17, when he entered the Erith Works of Vickers Ltd. as an engineering pupil-apprentice. At the same time Pierson attended evening classes to earn his bachelor of science degree in engineering. After his apprenticeship he stayed on with Vickers as a technician in its newly formed Aircraft Division. Just four years before becoming chief designer, he learned to fly on the company's monoplanes at the Vickers Flying School at Brooklands.

When the London drawing offices were shut down in 1919, Pierson took a small nucleus of the most promising staff to Brooklands. Remaining there as chief designer until 1945, he was responsible for the design of a long series of Vickers aircraft and a staff that grew from some two dozen in 1919 to more than 500 at the end of the World War II. In addition to the Vimy, aircraft produced under his leadership included the Viking amphibian, Virginia bomber, Victoria and Valentia transports, all-metal Viastra and Vellore transports, Vildebeest general-purpose military biplane, and Wellesley and Wellington bombers.

In 1945 Pierson became chief engineer of the whole Vickers-Armstrongs Aviation Group. When the war ended, he inspired the design team to produce the Viking airliner, and in 1946 he initiated the development of the Viscount, the world's first turboprop airliner. When Pierson retired he had served Vickers for nearly 40 years, his entire working career, with outstanding success. He played such a significant role that for many years it was said he *was* Vickers Aviation. Pierson died in January 1948, at age 56.

20

my Commercial flown by
ley Cockerell leaves
and in the race for the
e. Flying a Vimy bomber,
e van Ryneveld and Quintin
d join the race less than
weeks later. Neither aircraft
pletes the journey.

1921

An airmail route is established between Baghdad, Iraq, and Cairo, Egypt, and from Cairo to London. Vimys of the Royal Air Force squadrons in Egypt carry the mail from the opening of the route in June 1921 through early 1926.

1924

By April, after four years in service, *The City of London*, the best-known Vimy Commercial, reaches the 107,950-mile mark. While operated by Instone Air Line, it flew from England to Paris, Brussels, and Cologne.

Vickers Sets up at Brooklands

By 1915 the Vickers aircraft factories at Erith and Crayford could no longer keep up with demand, and a new works was founded at Brooklands. Aircraft production on a small scale began in April, but by 1917 the factory had to be expanded twice. A year later it was turning out 36 S.E.5a single-seat fighters per week, an output exceeding that of any other single British airplane factory.

In June 1917 Britain's Air Board issued Specification A.3.b, for a multi-engine, three-seat night bomber able to carry 3,000 pounds of bombs and bomb gear over a range of 300 miles at an altitude of 6,000 feet and at a speed of 80 to 85 miles per hour. The board then decided that night bombing was less accurate than day bombing and postponed all orders. After Major J. S. Buchanan, controller of the Technical Department, protested, the board reversed its decision, ordering 100 Handley Page night

bombers and three experimental prototypes each from the Handley Page and Vickers companies. Vickers gave its design the type number F.B.27. The design team was led by chief designer Rex Pierson.

Pierson's experience working on earlier Vickers twin-engine airplanes (page 229) undoubtedly proved valuable when he came to design the F.B.27. The first F.B.27 flew only three and a half months after the contract was placed, a considerable feat even for a large company such as Vickers. The prototype for the F.B.27 was begun when the earlier E.F.B.15 was under construction, and it is quite possible that some E.F.B.15 components were incorporated in the new bomber.

The Vimy Goes into Production

Powered by two 200-horsepower Hispano-Suiza V8 engines and spanning 68 feet, the first F.B.27 prototype made its maiden flight at Joyce Green on November 30, 1917, piloted by Gordon Bell. Manufacturer's trials led to alteration of the frontal radiators and replacement of the original hazardous exhaust stacks, which extended upward through the top wing, by horizontal pipes. Official trials showed that the F.B.27, which was only about two-thirds the size of a Handley Page O/100, could lift a greater load on little more than half the power and had "very good" maneuverability.

The two succeeding prototypes differed in various details and powerplant. The second, or Mk II, with Sunbeam Maori engines, was destroyed in a crash. The third, or Mk III, with the Fiat A.12bis engines originally intended

TOP: The first prototype Vimy, B9952, on the company's airfield at Joyce Green, Kent, in late 1917. Note the exhaust stacks passing through the upper wing (not popular with the military!), two-bladed propellers, shutterless radiators, and horn-balanced elevators. The B9952 lacked fixed fins in front of the rudders. It was later rebuilt and fitted with Salmson engines.

CENTER: The second prototype Vimy, B9953, Vimy Mk II, had inversely tapered plain

ailerons, plain unbalanced elevators, a ventral gun position in the fuselage, and 230-horsepower Sunbeam Maori engines with revised fuel and cooling systems.

BOTTOM: The third Vimy prototype, B9954, after the plain ailerons had been replaced by balanced ones. It had Fiat A.12bis engines with octagonal radiators. The design was approved for production as the Vimy Mk III with Fiat engines.

The Spirit of Brooklands

by **Peter McMillan** Although Brooklands had one of the first purpose-built motor-racing tracks, it somewhat accidentally became a spawning ground for early aviators from all across Europe. Once the first pioneers had set up shop there in 1908, a year after the racing track was built, others soon followed. From then through the end of its active days in motor racing and aircraft production, Brooklands was an unusual place for its ability to provoke both sides of the human mind: emotion and intellect.

Brooklands combined the thrill of speed with painstaking calculus; it was a place to dare and a place to cogitate. These often opposing forces met at Brooklands to drive world records and unimaginable inventions, including the Vickers Vimy and the Concorde.

In the early days, a congress of ideas happened at the simple Bluebird Cafe, located in the infield, which author Percy Rowe described as a "Parliament…yet one of the most exclusive clubs in Britain. Entrance demanded unselfishness, daring, camaraderie, zest."

Breaking records at Brooklands involved sacrifice, and many paid the ultimate price. One was Captain Ross Smith, one of the characters who inspired the building of the Vimy replica and the reliving of her original expeditions. Smith died here with his faithful mechanic Jim Bennett. But risk has never dissuaded those eager for real progress.

Brooklands was where dreamers dreamed and then carried out the practical work of building the long bridge from dream to reality. Few places can celebrate these distinct energies, which are the basis for human achievement.

Sopwith and other aviation pioneers established themselves in simple wooden sheds that became known as the Brooklands Flying Village.

for production machines, crashed and exploded while taking off with a bomb load. This did not deter officialdom, and in March 1918, the name "Vimy" was bestowed upon the F.B.27. The official system then in use required that a three-seat bomber built by Vickers be named after a French town beginning with *U* or *V*. The name "Versailles" was considered but fortunately not adopted; it would hardly have been appropriate in 1919 to have a serving bomber named after the venue of a peace conference.

In the first production contract, Fiat or Liberty engines were specified. Shortly thereafter the 360-horsepower Eagle VIII was added to the list, and the Vimy was set to become the standard night bomber for the Royal Air Force (RAF) and be used as well for antisubmarine work, equipping 24 squadrons. Eight subcontractors were also given orders. Engine supply problems slowed production, and two more prototypes were ordered, one with Eagles. The second was destroyed by fire before it flew.

Eleven Vimy Squadrons were to be deployed with the Independent Air Force of the RAF starting in May 1919, but the Armistice of November 1918 put an end to these plans. Many Vimy contracts, for a total of more than 1,000 aircraft, were severely curtailed or canceled. Limited production continued, however, and some 235 production Vimys were built. The first were not delivered until February 1919. No Vimys were used in the antisubmarine role, and the Eagle VIII became standard.

In July 1919 the Vimy entered service in its intended bomber role with the RAF. The first were ferried by air to 58 Squadron in Egypt, which, renumbered 70 Squadron in 1920, retained its Vimys until November 1922. Vimys, a mainstay of RAF activities in the Middle East, served as both bombers and transports, and 216 Squadron at Heliopolis retained them until 1926. With this squadron, the Vimy also flew on the demanding Cairo-Baghdad airmail route (page 230).

Interest in the UK in having a heavy-bomber component in the RAF was revived in 1922, and 7 Squadron became the first to be wholly equipped with Vimys in the peace-

TOP LEFT: Rolls-Royce Eagles powered the fourth Vimy prototype, F9569. It had rudders of greater area. Fuel capacity was increased to 452 Imperial gallons by reducing internal bomb stowage.

TOP RIGHT: This typical interwar RAF Vimy was with F Flight of No. 4 Flying Training School at Abu Sueir, Egypt. The engine cowlings were frequently left off to aid cooling in hot climates.

CENTER LEFT: Vimy H5070 in the Westland Aircraft Company factory at Yeovil, Somerset, in 1918. It was one of a batch of 75 ordered from the company, but only the first 25 were delivered, the remainder being canceled in September 1919.

BOTTOM: Four Vimys of 216 Squadron fly over Heliopolis race course, Cairo, Egypt, in 1928. By this time, the Vimy was at the end of its RAF career.

time service, using them until 1927. Three more Vimy squadrons were created in 1924, and the type also saw service with 502 (Ulster) Squadron in Northern Ireland, the first Special Reserve unit.

During the General Strike of 1926, Vimys distributed newspapers, mainly the *British Gazette*, published by the government. While performing this duty in very bad weather, a large number of pilots of 9 Squadron, based at Manston in Kent, became lost and delivered their papers at "diverse unintended destinations." The commanding officer spent a long time writing the requested report explaining why his squadron could not navigate properly.

When the type was superseded in its bomber role by the larger Vickers Virginia, the Vimy was used for training at home and abroad. As well as serving as dual-control pilot trainers, Vimys performed valuable work as parachute trainers. Before takeoff the trainee parachutists, two per aircraft, wearing both main and reserve parachutes, mounted small platforms in front of the rearmost outer interplane struts. With no safety belts, they stood and faced rearward, clutching the struts, while the aircraft taxied out, took off, and climbed to the dropping height. When the instructor in the Vimy's nose gave the signal, the parachutists performed a "pull-off"—they repositioned themselves behind the struts and then pulled the parachute ripcord. They then waited for the parachute to deploy and yank them off the wing.

In his 1972 book *Flying Between the Wars*, Air Commodore Allen Wheeler recalled: "The average interval of 4 seconds was quite long enough for some rather nervous trainees to conclude that the parachute had not opened and they therefore took a firm hold of the strut with both hands just before they were forcibly, but unwillingly, dragged away from it by the parachute. In one recorded case a somewhat muscular trainee clung on so strongly that the strut was

TOP LEFT: Vimy F8634 began life with Eagle engines but was fitted with dual controls and Bristol Jupiter air-cooled radial engines when it was reconditioned as a trainer in 1927. It is seen here at Brooklands after modification.

TOP RIGHT: Some Vimys were later painted in RAF night bombers' dark green Nivo dope scheme and given two-color red-and-blue roundels. This one, F9157, served with No. 6 Flying Training School at Manston in 1921.

CENTER: Six parachutists performed synchronized "pull-offs" from three Vimys during the 1929 Royal Air Force Display at Hendon.

BOTTOM: One of the Vimy's last duties in the RAF was serving as parachute trainer. After the aircraft gained altitude, the intrepid parachutists pulled the ripcords, and the parachutes pulled them off the wing.

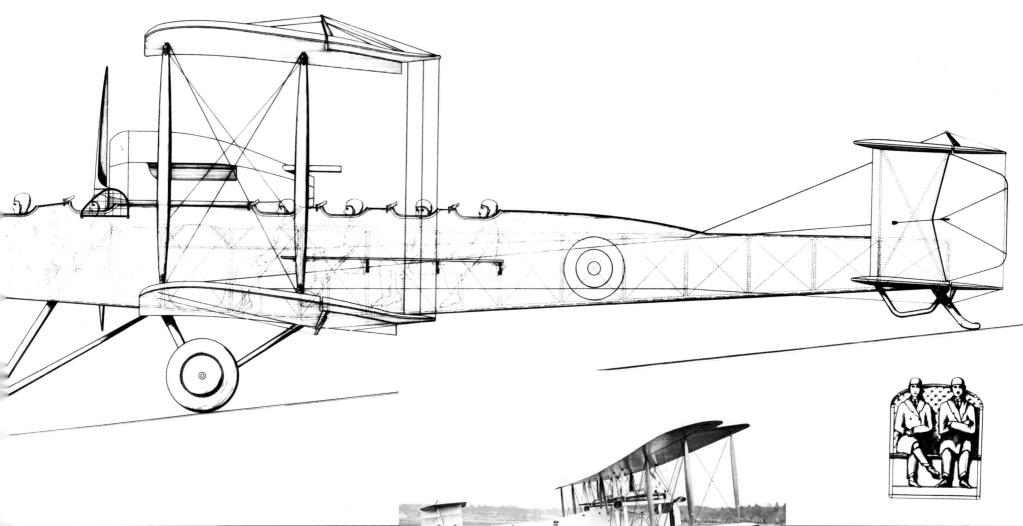

pulled out of its socket and the trainee landed on the aerodrome still clutching it. The Vimy managed to fly on and land. In several other cases the trainees would cling to the strut long enough for the Vimy to be pulled round into an unwilling turn before the parachute trainee's strength gave way and he was pulled off like a reluctant parasite."

The Vimy as Commercial Pioneer

In 1919 and 1920, the Vimy won undying fame in a role for which it had never been intended—that of trailblazer. John Alcock and Arthur Whitten Brown's nonstop transatlantic flight from Newfoundland to Ireland on June 14–15 in a converted Vimy heralded an age of intercontinental and transcontinental long-distance flying. A Vimy was also the chosen mount of Ross and Keith Smith when they embarked on their epic flight from England to Australia in November 1919, and of Pierre van Ryneveld and Quintin Brand for their laborious and troubled flight to the Cape in 1920.

TOP: A Vimy "Atlantic" type converted for commercial use. Eight passengers were to be accommodated in four two-seat open cockpits, and a ninth was seated in the nose.

ABOVE LEFT: John Alcock and Arthur Whitten Brown's Vimy at Brooklands immediately after completion, before the wheels beneath the nose were removed. The amidships gunner's position was removed to allow more fuel tanks to be accommodated in the fuselage.

LEFT: Unlike the transatlantic machine, the Vimy flown to Australia by Ross and Keith Smith was much closer to a standard Vimy, retaining the nose skid of service aircraft.

The prototype Vimy Commercial made its bulky presence felt at the First Air Traffic Exhibition at Amsterdam in August 1919. The monocoque fuselage accommodated 10 passengers.

The prototype Vimy Commercial, K-107, with the original round windows in its passenger cabin. It first flew on April 13, 1919.

Shortly after the Alcock and Brown flight, a drawing was prepared of a "Vimy 'Atlantic' Type converted for commercial use." It depicts a Vimy fuselage with four open passenger cockpits aft of the pilot's cockpit, each seating two passengers side by side. An additional passenger sits in the nose. Fortunately this nine-passenger freak remained unbuilt. It would surely have been unpopular with fare payers, who would rightly have expected better protection from the elements for their outlay.

Instead, Vickers greatly enhanced the type's civilian potential by replacing the conventional Vimy fuselage with a rotund oval-section wooden monocoque fuselage. This fuselage was married to standard Vimy wings and powerplant to create the Vimy Commercial, one of the first purpose-designed airliners. The pilot and copilot

were still unprotected in the open cockpit high on the nose, but the 10 passengers were completely enclosed in the fuselage and had windows on the outside world. In the rear fuselage and beneath the cockpit were 300 cubic feet of luggage space. Configuration as a mailplane was also possible, and it was suggested that mailbags might be dropped by parachute at chosen points en route.

The prototype, first registered K-107 and then G-EAAV, made its maiden flight at Joyce Green on April 13, 1919, piloted by Stanley Cockerell, who later used it for an unsuccessful attempt to fly to Cape Town. It was followed by three production aircraft. One was shipped to China as the first of an order for 100 to be used to set up an airline network. Ultimately only 40 of these were built, and the last two were not delivered. In 1921 a mail service

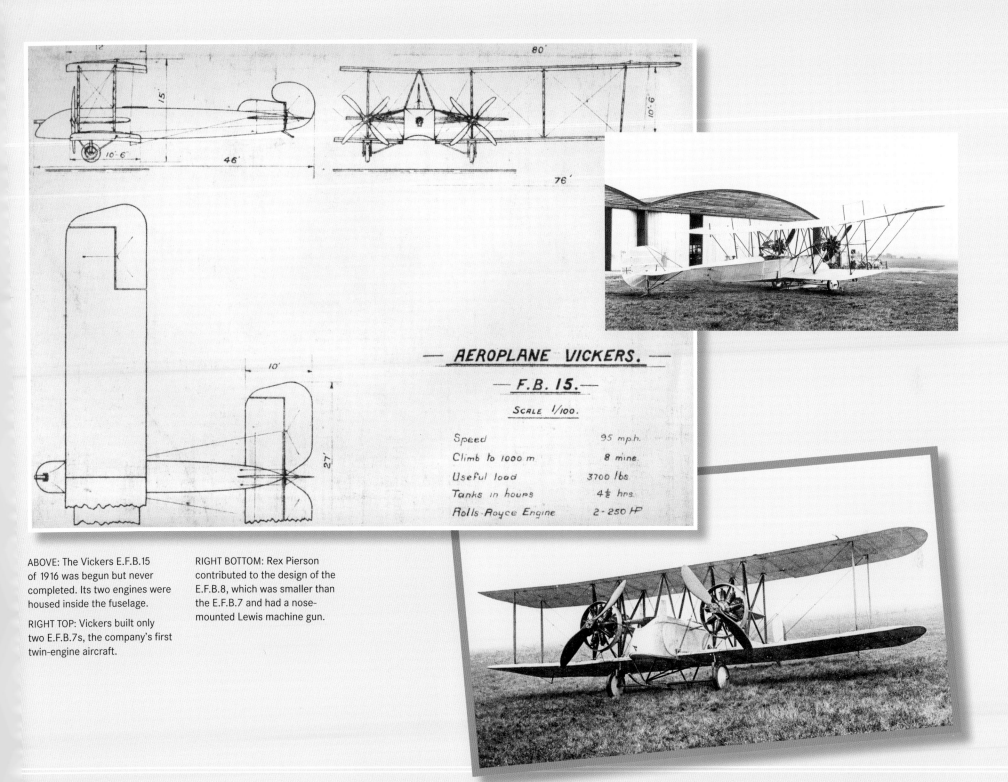

— AEROPLANE VICKERS. —

— F.B. 15. —

SCALE 1/100.

Speed	95 m.p.h.
Climb to 1000 m	8 mins.
Useful load	3700 lbs
Tanks in hours	4½ hrs.
Rolls-Royce Engine	2 - 250 HP

ABOVE: The Vickers E.F.B.15 of 1916 was begun but never completed. Its two engines were housed inside the fuselage.

RIGHT TOP: Vickers built only two E.F.B.7s, the company's first twin-engine aircraft.

RIGHT BOTTOM: Rex Pierson contributed to the design of the E.F.B.8, which was smaller than the E.F.B.7 and had a nose-mounted Lewis machine gun.

The Vimy's Predecessors

Before Vickers conceived the Vimy, it had built two previous twin-engine airplanes and started a third. The first was Experimental Fighting Biplane No. 7 (E.F.B.7) of 1915, which had the pilot located behind the wings and a gunner in the nose. Next came the smaller E.F.B.8 of late 1915, a redesign by Rex Pierson. Only two E.F.B.7s and one E.F.B.8 were built.

Then, in mid-1916, the War Office asked Vickers to construct an aircraft to carry an Ordnance C.F. two-pounder shell-firing gun weighing 800 pounds. This machine, the E.F.B.15, was to be the biggest Vickers airplane up to that time. Spanning 80 feet and having a useful load of 3,700 pounds, it was to be powered by two 250-horsepower Rolls-Royce Eagle engines housed within the fuselage, driving two propellers.

Construction of one of the two E.F.B.15s ordered was begun in the company's works at Bexley Heath in Kent, where experimental aircraft were built, in August 1916. Unfortunately Vickers found that "the further we progressed with this type the less it showed signs of being a success, as even for an aeroplane this was an extremely experimental proposition." The company repeatedly called for cancellation of the aircraft, which came about on November 6, 1917.

The Cairo-Baghdad Airmail

In March 1921 a bold decision was made to open a military desert air route. The flying distance from Cairo, Egypt, to Baghdad, Iraq, the final route, was roughly 860 miles, so a good number of emergency landing and refueling points had to be provided. As these would be almost impossible to find by navigation alone, a track had to be marked for the aircraft to follow. Helped by reconnoitering aircraft, two car convoys and a Fordson tractor were used to mark a track between Amman, Jordan, and Ramadi, Iraq, and then over the whole route. Landing grounds were marked at an average distance of 20 miles.

When the route opened, on June 23, pairs of aircraft left from either end once a fortnight. The first consignment of official airmail departed Baghdad for London on the July 28 flight and reached its destination on August 9. Two months later the mail service opened to the public.

The Vimys of 216 Squadron and the Vernons of 70 and 45 Squadrons operated the service with unfailing regularity until early 1926, when 70 Squadron's new Victorias took over. The route was flown in fair and foul weather, intense heat and bitter cold, as part of the squadrons' normal duties. The mail was practically never late.

Apart from engine failures and technical problems, the heavily loaded aircraft had difficulty rising from Amman in hot weather because it was some 2,600 feet above sea level. In summer the reduced air density made the height equivalent to 4,000 or 5,000 feet. The reduced rate of climb left a slender safety margin. Even when a slightly lower site at Ziza was used, it was often impossible to climb over the surrounding hills after 10 or 11 a.m. in summer. Winter rain and what was described as the "peculiar elusive lighting of the desert" could make the track hard to spot. The Vernons with their Eagle engines and big fuselages had several mishaps when aircraft either failed to get off or were caught in down-currents and had insufficient rate of climb to rise above them. Fitting of the more powerful Lion engines solved this problem. At the start of 1927, the route was taken over by Imperial Airways.

ABOVE: Vimy Ambulance J6855 was powered by a pair of Napier Lion engines. Steps were incorporated in the hinge-down entry door, and the appropriate red cross was painted on the fuselage.

LEFT: Vickers Vimy Ambulance J7143 of 45 Squadron over Hinaidi, Iraq, with the red cross incorporated inside the fuselage roundel.

BELOW: Vimy Commercial G-EASI *City of London* with its "Instone Blue" fuselage and silver wings.

between Peking (now Beijing) and Tsinan was begun, but in the war-torn China of the 1920s the Vimy Commercials found more use as hastily converted bombers. By April 1924 the Peking authorities had about 28 Vimys, some of which had locally made bomb racks. About 20 Vimy Commercials were converted as bombers by order of Chihli warlord Cao Kun and used in the second Chu-Feng war. Some Vimys survived in China as late as 1928.

The most famous Vimy Commercial was the 41st, G-EASI *City of London*, which faithfully served S. Instone & Co. and Imperial Airways from 1920 to 1926. It flew between Croydon, Paris, Brussels, and Cologne, and by July 1921 had logged 360 flying hours and carried 10,600 passengers. By April 1924, when Imperial took over, it had flown 107,950 miles. The 42nd aircraft went to France, and the 43rd and final machine was given high-lift wings and Napier Lion engines, thus essentially becoming the prototype of the Vernon. In 1922 it went to the Soviet Union, and two years later the Red Air Fleet lent it to the Russian airline Dobrolet.

Five Vimy Commercials with Lion engines were adapted for use as ambulances by the RAF. Each could accommodate four standard Royal Army Medical Corps stretchers, or eight sitting patients and two attendants. A nose hatch permitted easy loading of stretchers and patients.

The ultimate direct development of the Vimy Commercial and Ambulance was the Vernon troop carrier, with room for 11 troops and three crew. The Mk Is, of which 20 were built, had Eagle engines; the 25 Mk IIs had Lions; the Mk IIIs had high-compression Lion IIIs and additional wing fuel tanks. The Vernon served with 45 Squadron and 70 Squadron from 1922 to early 1927 in the Middle East, where the Mk Is had their Eagles replaced by Lions. They played a prominent role in the world's first air evacuation by lifting threatened British forces and civilians in Iraq from Sulaimaniya to Kirkuk in 1922. In 1923 Vernons flew some 480 troops to the threatened garrison at Kirkuk in history's first major military airlifting of troops. They were also used for supply dropping and medical evacuation missions.

Some traces of the original Vimy were retained in the Lion-powered Victoria troop carrier. This had a much longer monocoque fuselage married to the wings of the Virginia bomber, the Vimy's successor. In its initial form, the Virginia's structural design was based on that of the Vimy, and some resemblances were evident, especially in the tail surfaces. The Victoria was then re-engined with Bristol Pegasus radials to become the Valentia. When the airframe was also replaced, in the mid-1930s, the last Vimy components disappeared.

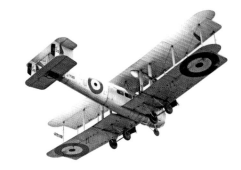

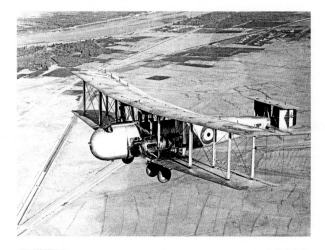

TOP: An unusual angle on Vernon J7135 in flight near Baghdad, Iraq. The original Vimy wings and tail surfaces are evident.

ABOVE CENTER: The Vickers Victoria had a longer fuselage than the Vernon and used the wings of the Vimy's successor, the Virginia bomber.

ABOVE: A newly completed Valentia at Brooklands in 1935 shows little remaining evidence of its Vimy origins apart from the tail surfaces.

VICKERS F.B.27 VIMY
Two 360-horsepower Rolls-Royce Eagle VIII Engines

This illustration depicts the standard RAF Vimy bomber of the 1920s. The Vimys used by Alcock and Brown and Ross and Keith Smith were structurally similar in most respects, but were modified for their long-distance flights, fitted with additional fuel tanks, and had none of the military equipment or armament.

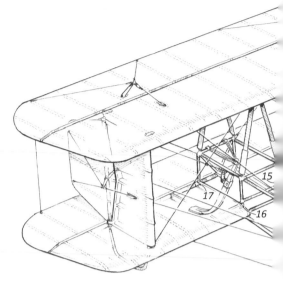

1	Spruce and plywood box section spars	35	Fuel fillers
2	Fabric binding	36	Fuel gravity tank (140 gal)
3	Hollow spruce struts	37	Fuel pipes
4	Two-bolt strut fitting	38	Prismatic fuel flow indicator
5	Lift wires heavier gauge than landing wires	39	Differential combined throttle control lever
6	Outer wing panel attachment plate	40	Cables to port and starboard engines
7	Steel tube engine-bearing struts	41	Both engines
8	Step	42	To synchronize
9	Ply and spruce ribs	43	Throttle and mixture control
10	Box-section compression ribs	44	Mk1 HAD bombsight
11	Steel tube front fuselage frame	45	Optional single or twin Lewis guns
12	Ply covering to aft cockpit	46	Magazine stowage
13	Fuselage top decking retaining straps	47	Center fuselage bays, originally bomb stowage, later additional fuel or flotation gear
14	Spruce sheet rolled tubes	48	Ventral gun position (0.303 in Lewis)
15	Steel tube rear section	49	Ventral gunner's observation window
16	Tailplane incidence adjustment	50	Underwing and underfuselage bomb stowage
17	Tailplane adjustment pivot	51	Fuzing and release panel, port rails
18	Aileron control	52	Fuzing and release panel, starboard rails
19	Aileron balance cable through tank	53	Wood-faired steel-tube undercarriage
20	Aileron control pulleys and access	54	Rubber bungee shock absorber
21	Cables to port and starboard rudders	55	Propeller guard (starboard side omitted)
22	360-hp Rolls-Royce Eagle VIII engine	56	Vickers propeller (10 ft, 5 in diameter)
23	Engine control and fuel pipe ducts	57	Altimeter
24	Engine RPM and temperature gauges	58	Airspeed indicator
25	Oil filler	59	Oil pressure gauges
26	Oil tank	60	Level
27	Water header tank	61	Magneto switches
28	Downpipes to radiator	62	Hand starter magneto
29	Radiator	63	Hand fuel pump
30	Adjustable louvers	64	Fuel cock
31	Generator	65	Ignition (advance and retard)
32	Fuel pump	66	Radiator shutter control
33	Forward fuel tank (85 gal)	67	Compass
34	Aft fuel tank (140 gal)		

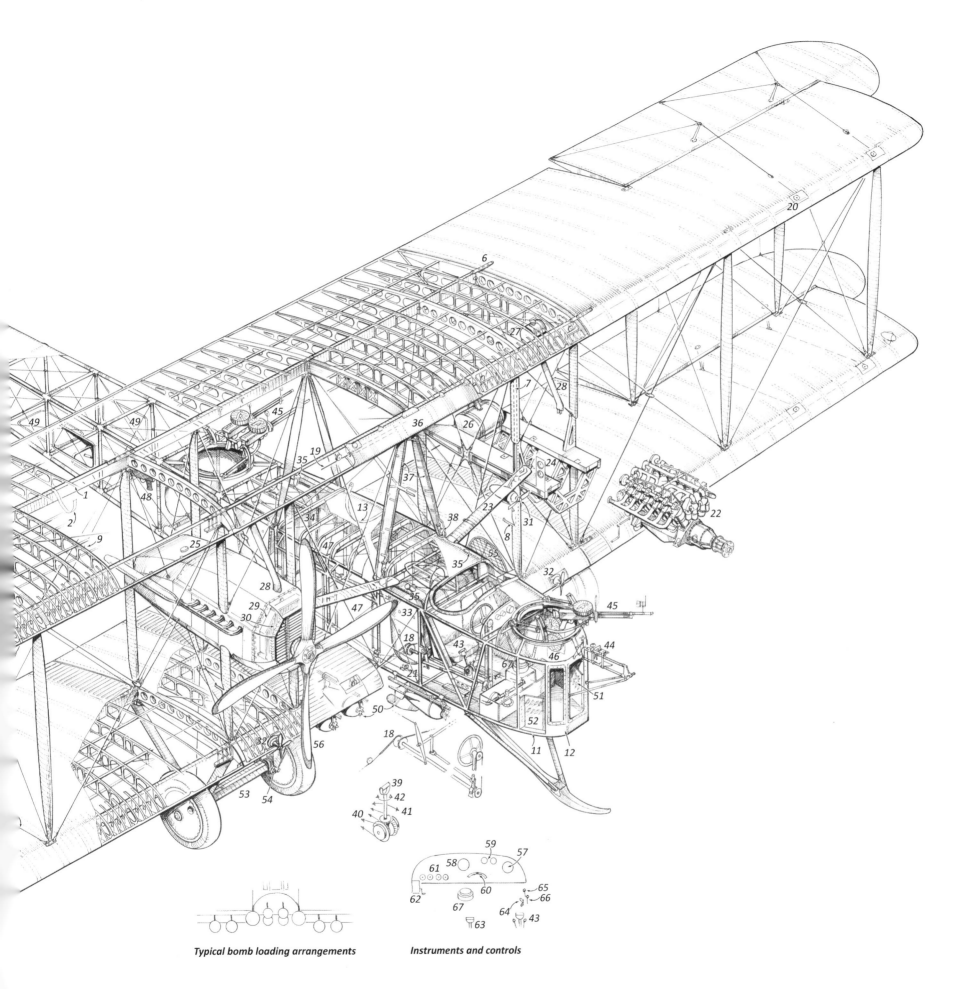

Typical bomb loading arrangements

Instruments and controls

BUILDING A TIME MACHINE

by John LaNoue Turning a large dream into a reality in a very short period of time usually requires risk, a large dose of naïveté, and a whole lot of capital. This project was no exception to these requirements. We would, in effect, have to replicate a Vimy factory, complete with the jigs, fixtures, patterns, and special-built machinery required to manufacture the actual aircraft parts. We eventually used 150 sheets of aircraft plywood, hundreds of board feet of dimensional lumber, 500 yards of grade A cotton fabric, 1,000 feet of steel tube, 700 feet of control cable, 300 gallons of dope and thinner, and 240 feet of ⅝-inch bungee cord. We tied 10,000 rib stitches and fabricated 330 feet of box spar, 300 leading edge ribs, 126 main wing ribs, and hundreds of metal fittings. The initial construction would consume about 30,000 man-hours of effort coordinated between two shops located half a planet apart—one in California, the other in Australia—over an 18-month period.

Replicating this ancient aircraft as true to the original as possible was our desire, but reliability and safety were also our objectives. We had to make a few concessions if we wanted to reenact the Vimy's epic flights. First, we hired Bill Whitney, an accomplished Australian aeronautical engineer and designer, to do a stress analysis based on data from the original Vickers drawings and to redraft the entire catalog of existing drawings from microfilm to easy-to-read CAD drawings. He also designed parts and created drawings to replace the many missing pages, and he designed necessary modifications when flaws and weaknesses were found in the original.

Maintaining visual authenticity was our main criterion when making any modifications to the aircraft's design. Modifications were limited to improving structural integrity, powerplant reliability, and safety. We made no changes to the airfoil or external dimensions.

Even though the art of aircraft design was still in its infancy in 1918, Bill's stress analysis determined that the Vickers engineers did a good job. Strengthening the spars on the upper center section and adding a few more compression ribs were the only modifications to the wings. The original fuselage frame had a lug-joined tubular-steel forward section and a wire-braced, wood-truss aft section. Bill's advice was to build the fuselage entirely of 4130 steel tube. This provided a lighter and stronger structure without changing the external visual lines and allowed us to install larger fuel tanks.

Bev and Lang Kidby, Peter McMillan, John LaNoue, Dan Nelson, and Tessa Barroll (from left) presented the completed Vimy at a rollout party on July 7, 1994, her first public viewing.

OPPOSITE LEFT: As the Vimy began to take shape in a hangar at the abandoned air base at Hamilton Field in Novato, California, the team fitted the wings and tail section to the fuselage.

OPPOSITE CENTER: John LaNoue and Peter McMillan rigged the undercarriage (top). Dan Nelson (bottom) tensioned the many bracing wires.

FAR LEFT TOP: A graceful bow made of 14 layers of birch aircraft plywood formed the leading-edge wingtip.

FAR LEFT BOTTOM: John LaNoue, Lang Kidby, and Peter McMillan (from left) first worked in a shop in Sonoma, California, where they laid out the framework of the Vimy before moving the pieces to Hamilton Field.

LEFT: John LaNoue installed one of the 140-pound propellers, produced in Australia from Tasmanian oak.

Originally the Vimy was designed as a single-pilot airplane with a one-position yoke and rudder bar, both located on the right side of the cockpit. Pulling back on the yoke to increase drag on the tail skid provided the only braking action during ground maneuvers. Our aircraft was outfitted with dual rudder bars, hydraulic brakes on the main gear, and a throw-over yoke that allowed the aircraft to be flown from either seat of the main cockpit. A locking tail wheel replaced the tail skid, so our aircraft could maneuver on modern paved runways. Negotiating the world's complex airspace also required the addition of modern radios and avionics.

As the original aircraft evolved, several different engines powered the Vimy. The most common and successful engine was the water-cooled, 20.5-liter, 360-horsepower Rolls-Royce Eagle. We could have obtained a pair of Eagles, but using them would have severely limited the safety and reliability of our operations. Spares would have been a problem, and the Eagle's to-basic-overhaul time was a mere 100 hours.

Modern aircraft powerplants also had their drawbacks. Strapping a pair of Pratt and Whitney R-985 radial engines would have been easy, but fitting them into the Vimy's distinctive cowlings (then known as power eggs) would have been impossible. Lycoming O-540s would have fit into the power eggs, but these engines would have needed reduction gears to swing the trademark 10-foot airscrews.

Because the long scimitar-shaped blades are one of the Vimy's notable features, we were unwilling to alter the massive, four-bladed twin propellers to accommodate higher-revving modern aircraft engines. Therefore, if we needed a reduction drive, we'd opt for an auto engine conversion. Over our Vimy's lifespan, we have operated with three different engine and propeller combinations, the last of which was our most successful.

Our first installation was based on a pair of fuel-injected cast-iron block Chevrolet 454-cubic-inch V8s with 4:1 planetary (epicyclic) reduction gearboxes built by Australian race car builder Wayne Daley. These Chevy engines successfully carried our Vimy from England to Australia, despite one mishap.

ABOVE: The team prepared to fit the engines and then installed the electrical and fuel systems.

ABOVE CENTER: Bev Kidby (top) was one of the volunteers who painstakingly stitched the fabric to the ribs. The process called for more than 10,000 knots, each requiring the right amount of tension. Attaching the tail of the Vimy (bottom) was one of the final tasks.

Our second engine/power train installation was based on a 5.4-liter aluminum block V12 that typically powers a modern European luxury sedan. This package was engineered by a team of ace mechanics led by engineer Dr. Christoph Hoerster and renowned engine builder Adolph Fischer, both based in Munich, Germany. The engines featured computer-controlled ignition and fuel injection, and a custom 5:1 planetary reduction drive matched to wooden propellers custom-fabricated by MT Propeller of Straubing, Germany. This package powered our airship across the mountainous and rugged terrain of Africa. After solving some problems associated with gearbox cooling, we continued using this installation over several sojourns around the United States.

Our third and most successful engine installation was also our most complicated. For this installation, we utilized an actual certified aircraft engine, the Orenda OE600.

This engine was newly certified and manufactured by Orenda Recip of Toronto, Canada. Its geometry and architecture were based somewhat on the big block Chevy. It featured a 500-cubic-inch displacement, water-cooled aluminum block V8, intercooled turbocharging, a dry sump oil system, an integral reduction gearbox, and a maximum power output of 600 horsepower. Complications installing these engines arose from, one, their sheer size and, two, the number of additional accessories associated with the oil system, turbocharger, radiator, intercooler, and ducting. The installation required an entirely new motor mount bearer frame as well as many alterations to the fuel and electrical systems.

We also had to adapt our beautiful wooden MT propellers from the V12s to the Orendas. Unfortunately, this could not be accomplished. The power-band of the Orendas was entirely out of sync with the fixed pitch of our propellers. On the advice of Gerd Mulbaur, president of MT Propeller, a new set of propellers was constructed. These large diameter, four-bladed, constant-speed propellers (not at all original to World War I aircraft) allowed for pitch change during flight, giving greater flexibility in the use of the Orendas' power. MT Propeller's offer of a partial sponsorship in constructing these new propellers persuaded us to choose the company's design, though it compromised the authenticity of our replica.

In the end, the new propellers looked great. Although they are constant speed and feature a metal hub that houses the mechanical parts, the blades themselves are wood and are painted in an authentic World War I color. The large diameter of the new propellers precluded us from using the full horsepower potential of the Orendas. Over a certain RPM range, the tip speed of the propellers breaks the sound barrier, which can damage the propellers as well as the pilots' eardrums. We were still able to exercise as much as 400 horsepower from the engines as well as getting the benefit of sea level performance from the engines at high altitude, due to the turbocharging. Operating the Orendas below their rated power output will also extend their service life.

Our Vimy was now the most powerful it had ever been. The additional performance proved extremely useful for the Atlantic flight, as an additional fuel capacity of 300 gallons was added to the airframe. One of the unforeseen benefits of the new propellers was the reduced noise. With the original Chevys and the V12s, the sound level produced by the engine

exhaust and props was equivalent to sitting alongside a dragster. Enduring such sound levels over long flights was physically fatiguing to the pilots and crew. With the new powerplant and propeller combination, we could operate the engines during cruise at lower RPM settings and still produce plenty of power while enjoying a lower noise level in the cockpit.

I think about all the life and earth that have passed beneath the Vimy's wings over the years. When it all began as nothing more than an idea in 1993, I could never have imagined the extent to which the Vimy's creation would influence so many lives. Many times the Vimy has been the anvil that has forged deep and lasting friendships, and only infrequently has she served as an object of fierce contention that has dissolved once close relationships. I could have never imagined how many hands would touch the airplane, how many eyes would see it, how many minds would be in awe of it, and how so many people would be inspired by it, all because a young Peter McMillan, a man possessed with infectious enthusiasm, had a desire to fulfill a dream.

ABOVE LEFT: Wayne Daley (left) and John LaNoue installed one of the original engines.

TOP: A truss customarily used for lifting stage scenery was employed to help install the upper wing.

ABOVE: John LaNoue, concentrating on the forward section of the aircraft, installed the wheel and flight controls and began working on the electrical system.

The Vimy replica came in for her first landing on July 30, 1994, after a partial power loss in the left engine.

TRANSPORTING THE VIMY

by John LaNoue Over the years, the Vimy proved herself a stout and intrepid world traveler as she has negotiated some of the most difficult terrain and weather conditions the world can serve up. Yet, several times the Vimy has traversed the planet as a passenger on another vessel rather than as the mighty Galleon of the Skies.

Desperate to make our launch date for the 1994 Australian expedition, we split the Vimy into two parts and removed the landing gear. The aircraft was then shoehorned into the cargo hold of a C-5 Galaxy and flown from Travis Air Force Base in California to Mildenhall AFB in the United Kingdom, courtesy of the US Air Force.

Twice the aircraft was completely dismantled and shipped in two 40-foot open-top shipping containers: the first time, from Australia in 1995, when she was returned to England after the Australian expedition, and the second, from Cape Town in 1999, following the African expedition, when she made her triumphant return to her birthplace in California.

After a succession of test flights, the Vimy was flown in August 1994 to Travis Air Force Base in Fairfield, California, for the trip to England on a C-5 Galaxy.

The Vimy's forward and aft sections, separated at the trailing edge of the wing, were carried onto the Galaxy by an Air Force vehicle specially designed for moving large equipment.

The Vimy arrived safely at Mildenhall Air Force Base in England. At slightly under 8,000 pounds, she was a relatively light load compared to other aircraft cargo.

e team was given an empty hangar at Mildenhall where they rked to reassemble the Vimy. The deadline for reaching nborough, departure point for the Australia flight, was coming.

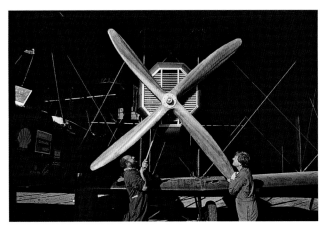

After a celebratory tour of Australia following the 1994 flight from England, the Vimy was stored at Kevin Weldon's farm, Luskintyre, north of Sydney.

In 1995, Peter McMillan, John LaNoue, and Erik Durfey joined Lang Kidby in Australia to make plans for bringing the Vimy back to the UK in preparation for the flight to Africa.

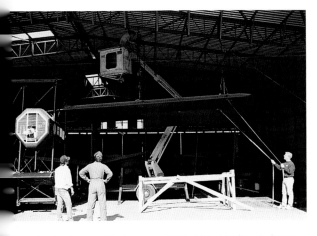

e again, the Vimy had to be disassembled for shipping. A cherry er was brought in to perform the heavy lifting.

An upper wing was lifted from the airplane. All the components were carefully examined, and those in need of attention noted for future repair.

The disassembled airplane was shoehorned into two open-top 40-foot shipping containers. One accommodated the fuselage.

McMillan sat in the forward seat after the fuselage was lly lowered into the container. The team worked for five long before the Vimy was ready to go.

Each container was placed on a truck for the trip to Sydney. It would take about eight weeks for the Vimy to reach England.

The pieces of the Vimy rose above the open-top containers. Despite the careful planning and packing, the team was always concerned about clearance.

FACTS & FIGURES

Miles Flown
39,100 estimated miles (including local flights and testing)

Hours in Air
920 hours

Amount of Gas Used
36,400 gallons

Highest Altitude
13,800 feet in Wiltshire, England

Worst Landings
Talangbatu, Sumatra (rice field)

Chyulu Hills, Kenya (dirt runway)

Slowest Flight
Pisa–Rome (aborted): Approximately 5 miles covered in 18 minutes at 16 knots

Longest Flights
Transatlantic:
18 hours and 19 minutes

Delhi–Calcutta:
10 hours and 10 minutes

Worst Food
Fish and chips in Hampshire, UK, pub made Lang Kidby grab the sick sack just before departure from Farnborough to Australia.

Vimy Specifications

	Replica NX-71MY	Original G-EAOU
Wingspan	68 ft.	same
Wing Chord	10 ft. 6 in.	same
Wing Area	1,376 sq. ft.	same
Length	43 ft. 6½ in.	same
Height	16 ft. 4 in.	same
Tailspan	16 ft.	same
Wheel Track	21 ft. 11 in. (outer)	same
	11 ft. 1 in. (inner)	same
Propeller (diameter)	10 ft. 8 in.	10 ft. 6 in.
Cruising Speed	85 mph	same
Stall Speed	45 mph	same
Weight (empty)	7,940 lb.	7,201 lb.
Weight (maximum)	12,499 lb.	12,500 lb.
Endurance	13.5 hours	11 hours
Fuel Capacity	673 gal.	516 gal.
Engines	454 cu. in. Chevrolet V8s	Rolls-Royce Eagle VIII V12s
	*5.4 liter BMW M73 V12s	
	**500 cu. in. Orenda OE600 V8s	

*Engines switched after Australia flight.
**Engines switched after Africa flight.

ENGLAND–AUSTRALIA

Countries where the replica Vimy landed (in sequence):

France
Italy
Greece
Egypt
Saudi Arabia
Bahrain
Oman
Pakistan
India
Myanmar
Thailand
Singapore
Indonesia
Australia

Flight Dates
Original: November 12–December 10, 1919

Replica: September 11–October 22, 1994

Total Hours Flown
Original: 135 hours, 55 minutes

Replica: 148 hours, 35 minutes

Total Miles en Route
Original: 11,060 miles

Replica: 11,234 miles*

Average Miles per Flying Day
Original: 461 miles

Replica: 450 miles

*Not including approximately 3,500 miles flown in Australia after arrival in Darwin.

ENGLAND–SOUTH AFRICA

Countries where the replica Vimy landed (in sequence):

Germany
France
Italy
Greece
Egypt
Saudi Arabia
Djibouti
Ethiopia
Kenya
Tanzania
Malawi
Zambia
Zimbabwe
South Africa

Flight Dates
Original: February 4–March 20, 1920

Replica: June 1–July 29, 1999

Total Hours Flown
Original: 132 hours, 12 minutes

Replica: 109 hours, 30 minutes**

Total Miles en Route
Original: 8,820 miles

Replica: 9,082 miles

Average Miles per Flying Day
Original: 365 miles

Replica: 284 miles

**Flight completed in a de Havilland D.H.9.

CANADA–IRELAND

Flight Dates
Original: June 14–June 15, 1919

Replica: July 2–July 3, 2005

Total Hours Flown
Original: 16 hours, 28 minutes

Replica: 18 hours, 19 minutes

Total Miles en Route
Original: 1,933 miles

Replica: 1,940 miles

A FLYING LESSON

by Peter McMillan When you walk up to the Vimy for your first flight, you can't help but be awed by the size of the machine. Stand by the wingtip, about head height for an average man. Look up, and you'll see the upper wing, way up there, more than 16 feet off the ground. Move the massive aileron up and down. It's the same size as the entire wing of a Cessna 172. Walk around the tail, and you'll think you're seeing double. There are two of everything: two rudders, two vertical fins, two elevators, two stabilizers. All the control cables are external, so the rear fuselage looks like a giant guitar. Time to mount up.

Athletic Entry

Rather than climb up the nose skid for our first entry, let's jump up on the trailing edge of the wing, next to the fuselage. It's a big step, but you can pull yourself up by grabbing the rim of the rear cockpit, then crawl up on the deck. Step down into the pilot's cockpit. Settle into the left seat and acquaint yourself with the instruments. The engine gauges will take some getting used to—they're about 6 feet away to your left, mounted out on the engine cowling. Put your seatbelt harness on first, then your helmet and goggles. Now let's go flying.

First, make sure that both throttles (the black, knobbed levers between the seats down by your right hand) are closed. Then, make sure the number one fuel tank is on: that's the first red lever from the left under your seat. Next, go to the left side of the panel and turn both master switches on, then the fuel pumps, and set the mixtures idle cutoff. The fuel pressure gauge should read 48 psi. If it does, push the big red button on the left to start the left engine. (This engine is usually started first, because the pilot has a clear view of the left side.)

Slowly advance the mixture, and the big V8 should bark to life after the propeller blades have made only a few turns past your ear. The engine should settle down to a nice rumble of about 1,100 RPM. Now yell "Clear right!" and repeat the procedure on that side. Check the oil pressure again. It should be about 65 psi. Let the radiator temp warm up to about 160° Fahrenheit. Make sure the tail wheel is unlocked. We're ready to taxi.

Use the throttles gingerly: weighing in at almost 10,000 pounds, the Vimy can't stop in a hurry. Keep your taxi speed down to a brisk walking pace. You can steer side to side by using differential power from the engines. Move the wheel and the rudders, and check the action of the

control surfaces. The Vimy is as heavy as you thought! Complete the preflight checks, and we'll be ready to line up on the runway.

Wiggle the rudders as you're rolling slowly forward, until you're happy with their alignment. Now, reach down with your right hand and lock the tail wheel. Bring the power in smoothly, and you'll be surprised to find you're barely moving forward, even with full throttle. We're picking up speed, so keep it straight with the rudders—very effective. Ease the control wheel forward about 2 inches to get the tail up, unless there's a passenger in the nose seat (in which case, hold back pressure throughout the takeoff or you may drag the nose skid). While we went over that, you probably didn't notice that we're in the air already!

Two-fisted Flying

We lifted off below 50 miles per hour, and now we're climbing at 400 feet per minute because we have only 200 gallons of fuel on board. Keep her climbing at 60 miles per hour, and don't attempt any turns yet, but see if you can synchronize the props. That's better: you can tell by the resonance beating on the side of your head. Level off at 1,500 feet and the airspeed will come up to 85 miles per hour. Ease the throttles back and crane your neck to check the engine gauges. The fuel pressure is stable, and the water temp has come up to 180° Fahrenheit. Okay.

Now try a shallow turn to the left. Lead with the rudders and move the wheel slightly left. Whoa! Not what you expected! The nose pitched up and to the right. Did you notice that nothing happened when you first used the ailerons? That null area is because all four ailerons are floating up about 2 inches at the trailing edges when the plane is in flight. So you get no response at first and then quite a bit when you roll the wheel into a turn.

Let me show you a trick. For a shallow right turn, let's use a touch of right aileron and plenty of left rudder. See how much easier that is. For a steeper turn, we'll start the same way and then roll in some left aileron to set a 30-degree bank to the left. There's the angle of bank; hold hard against it—harder! Don't let that bank steepen—the plane is dynamically unstable. This means that once displaced in any direction she will continue to move in that direction and will keep right on going unless you hold against the bank. Now lead with the right rudder to level the wings. She feels like an old mare, doesn't she? You can nudge her hard, but she still doesn't move in a hurry.

Back to Earth

There's a slight breeze from the west, so we must land into it as much as possible. Turn downwind, and don't be alarmed, but if you get a gust on the tail, she'll feel like you've lost control. You're okay. It's just that the null area of the ailerons is much larger when a wind comes from behind. Use the controls aggressively. Although the Vimy is large, she is very slow, so she doesn't need a lot of space to land.

Set up at 60 to 65 miles per hour and ease the power back to about 1,800 RPM. Much quieter, right? Listen to the music of the wires. The props are only at 850 RPM. You can almost count the blades. We are abeam the runway's numbers at 800 feet, floating down at 300 feet per minute. It's better to make a continuous shallow turn rather than a square turn to final approach. Don't let her drift across the centerline.

Alignment looks good. At 300 feet, start easing off the power. You are gliding in a giant box kite. Use the rudders to pick up that wing drop. Over the numbers...now begin a gradual roundout. Keep the wheel coming back slowly, a few feet to go. Isn't it incredible how she floats! It's the ground effect from the massive wings. Forget about the airspeed indicator. Concentrate on attitude. Nose up a bit more, with the wheel in your lap. Whump! She's on all the tires at once: a perfect five-point landing. Keep her straight. Tap-dance on those rudders. Slow her down—the right engine will turn her off the runway. Watch your arms when waving to your friends (those props are close). Shut off the switches, and be careful climbing out—it's a long drop to the ground. Jump off the wing, and take off your helmet. God 'Elp All Of Us—you're a Vimy pilot!

THE VIMY RETIRES

by Peter McMillan On November 15, 2009, we set out on what would be the last flight of the beloved Vickers Vimy. She had clocked nearly a thousand hours spanning the globe, and dozens of times she could have permanently ended our adventures. But it was time for her to go home, to Brooklands, where she would live alongside so many other great aircraft of the past, the Sopwith Camel, the Wellington, the Concorde.

John Dodd, Clive Edwards, and I departed Dunsfold for the last sortie, a mere 23 miles. The late autumn sun was brilliant as we circled the Brooklands Museum site. I peered over the side to survey the remaining parts of the racetrack banking, crumbling but speaking volumes of the past. Just beyond the section of track near Byfleet village, I saw the spot where Ross Smith crashed to his death in 1922. Then I knew clearly this was the right time and the right place to bring her back to earth for the last time. I had no feelings of melancholy.

We rolled gently onto the short grass strip adjacent to the museum at about 3:45 p.m. to an enthusiastic crowd of a thousand or so. With dusk nearing, the sky quickly turned a shade of antique amber. Walking away from the Vimy, I looked back to see a few onlookers touching her fabric gently or plucking her wires. I thought about the words of Ross Smith in his article in *National Geographic* magazine. He wrote of the Vimy being "the zenith of man's constructional genius, the closest thing to animate life we have created." This may seem an overstatement, but think about where tomorrow's pioneers might take us 50 years from now.

For me, the Vimy project simply represented my dreams as a young boy come to life, dreams of time travel, far-off adventure, danger and action, heroes and villains, dreams of meeting the elements and prevailing. How wonderful it will be when a child comes to Brooklands, looks up at our well-worn flying machine, at the maze of wires and the patches in the fabric, and the magical cycle begins again.

THE PLAYERS

PETER McMILLAN was raised in North Carolina and at age eight visited Kitty Hawk, North Carolina, site of the Wright brothers' first powered flight. He built models, occasionally peeked through airport fences, and spent much of his youth reading and dreaming of the "knights of the air." Eventually, in the early 1980s, Peter took up work in California and in his spare time became involved with a group devoted to restoring and flying antique aircraft. Peter was mentored by a true veteran, Harry Munson, a modest man who always had time for those willing to learn the right way. Harry, an example for all fliers, showed that success in aviation is defined not by what you have but by what you know. In 1990 Peter flew a 1942 Harvard (AT-6) trainer from England to Australia, which rekindled his youthful dreams of far-off adventure.

In 1992 Lang Kidby and Peter conceived the Vimy project, which sidelined his career in finance but allowed him to fulfill another dream, living and writing a great adventure for *National Geographic*, which featured it on the cover in May 1995. The story was shared with millions through the magazine and more personally through illustrated lectures at numerous venues, including the Royal Geographical Society in London. Peter's first book, *The Greatest Flight*, retells the Vimy journeys to Australia, past and present, and is well illustrated by Jim Stanfield's memorable images. It was, in all respects, the dream of a young boy come true. However, the unpaid bills of the Vimy project cut short his career as an adventurer. Returning to the business realm, Peter was very fortunate to land at TPG Capital, a global investment firm. Amid other priorities, he still enjoys pleasure aloft in a 1964 Beech Super 18.

LANG KIDBY cannot recall ever being interested in indoor activities. His family loved travel and doing "different" things, and when he was old enough, he began organizing his own adventures with school pals into the rainforest mountains behind Australia's Gold Coast. Anything mechanical caught Lang's interest: His first vehicle was a World War II army truck that he drove on the deserted beaches of Stradbroke Island at age 14. At age 16, he took four-wheel-drive adventures into the outback with a school pal, and at 17, he worked on desert oil rigs. By the time Lang was 17, he owned his own interstate semitrailer. After 15 years as an Australian Army pilot, including six years in New Guinea, Lang owned a marine construction business complete with tugs and barges.

Aviation has always been prominent in Lang's activities. He organized the England to Australia World Vintage Air Rally in 1990, partnered with Peter McMillan on the Vimy project, and restored and flew a 1927 Avro Avian biplane solo from England to Australia. Later, he drove a hundred-year-old Itala motorcar 15,000 kilometers from Peking to Paris via Mongolia and Siberia. Next, he and his wife, Bev, completed a circumnavigation from Vladivostok to Anchorage in a baby 1969 Fiat 500 car, the smallest vehicle ever to have circled the world. Lang's piloting skills were critical to the Vimy project. Perhaps even more critical was his ability to chop through, or ignore, jungles of red tape across the world. Lang's fortitude, in particular, lifted the Vimy from her crash site in Sumatra, a scene that to the less determined would have surely looked like an early end to the project.

JOHN LaNOUE was born and raised in Northern California. At age three, he discovered that by using pieces of discarded sandpaper he could sharpen points on small sticks, which could be used as crude tools or weapons. This epiphany kindled a lifelong fascination for making wondrous and useful things. When John was six, he became obsessed with unlocking the mysterious knowledge contained in books. For the next 12 years, he lived in books—books on adventure, history, tools, construction, boats, science fiction, airplanes, guns, fishing, and hunting. John also honed his skills with tools and their use in shaping wood and metal. He built many things, including several small boats.

At age 18, he escaped the confines of a government education and fled to Latin America, where he lived and traveled in exile for a year and learned the art of wood sculpting. Upon returning to the United States, he launched his career as a sculptor and industrial artist. John has spent most of his adult life working in the theater and film industries, doing set construction and special effects work. John developed a fascination for flying late in life, at age 32. His affliction has been diagnosed as chronic and incurable. In addition to leading the original construction team in building the Vimy replica (which took nearly 30,000 man-hours), John completed the two subsequent engine retrofits largely on his own. He also served time in the "gondola," as the Vimy cockpit was originally called, when he flew as copilot from England to South Africa in 1999.

MARK REBHOLZ cannot remember a time when he wasn't enthralled with aviation. As a child, he read every aviation-related book in school libraries and imagined himself flying alongside his heroes as they pioneered airmail routes, navigated the oceans, and flew passengers and cargo through heavy weather. Mark started his first flying lessons—in gliders—at the age of 13. By the time he was a young adult, he had his commercial pilot certificate and was earning a living as a pilot. During the last years of the Vietnam War, he flew as a boom operator on KC-135s in the US Air Force and was introduced to airborne celestial navigation.

Over the years, Mark has flown as a mail pilot in well-worn Beech 18s and earned captain's stripes as a pilot for United Airlines. He has always sought out interesting work as a pilot, a mechanic, and even a celestial navigator, flying vintage aircraft and participating in numerous aviation events and projects as a volunteer. Mark was critical to all of the Vimy expeditions in numerous respects—flight ops manager, logistics coordinator, support plane pilot, mechanic, diplomat, navigator, and chief pilot for two of the three intercontinental voyages. Today, Mark earns his living as a tanker pilot, dropping fire retardant on wildland fires for the Bureau of Land Management in the western United States.

PETER McBRIDE is a bit of an adventure nut. Whether it involves antique aviation, climbing, surfing, or just a good trek through a remote corner of the globe, Peter is keen. He thanks his parents for this brimming wanderlust, as they had a tendency to drag him on daunting jaunts when he was a young boy. His first big outing? Climbing Mt. Kenya at the age of 10 with his parents. After graduating Dartmouth College, Peter turned to photography and writing as a way to document and share his passion for foreign and remote lands, no matter how distant. Africa has always been close to Peter's heart, but he has had the good fortune to work in more than 50 countries and fly in a vast variety of aircrafts for scores of publications around the world.

On the London to Cape Town flight in 1999, Peter was the photographer and so much more. His efforts and those of his Kenya-based friends made it possible to clear the seemingly insurmountable mountains (and mountains of red tape to get from Djibouti across Ethiopia into Kenya). His story and photos of the Africa flight were published in the May 2000 *National Geographic*. Peter is a contributing photographer for *National Geographic Traveler* and the former *Adventure* magazines. His latest work employs the aerial perspective in a book: *The Colorado River—Flowing Through Conflict*. When not on assignment, he can be found in the mountains or on the rivers around Basalt, Colorado. He also might be working on his three-point landings in a Piper SuperCub.

DAVID R. HOLBROOKE and Vimy's nature are best captured by the following description: "this grey spirit yearning in desire to follow knowledge like a sinking star beyond the utmost bounds of human thought." The phrase was given to David in his high school yearbook, but resurfaced in his mind when he discovered the

Vimy and met its impassioned crew in 1997 following the hugely successful 1994 flight from England to Australia. David's passion for adventure soon enveloped him, along with his family, his friends, and his staff, in all subsequent Vimy adventures, including the flights from England to South Africa and from San Francisco to Oshkosh, and the final flights from San Francisco to Newfoundland and then to Ireland and England.

Affectionately called "The Fueller" by his Vimy cohorts, David worked tirelessly (as did all true Vimy-ites) to complete the arduous, complex, and expensive adventures. When others doubted the outcome of a thorny problem, be it engines, insurance, or plain old money, David would first buoy the Vimy team and then bear down and divine a solution to the crisis du jour.

David's American, Canadian, and British ancestry resonated closely with Vimy's and served both well until the Vimy was finally brought home to rest at her birthplace in the Brooklands Museum at the site of the Vickers factory in Surrey, England, where the original Vimys were born. His background as a physician, entrepreneur, venture capitalist, and general troublemaker served him well with the Vimy project; the uplifting energy of the machine inspired him to devote his own energy to spreading the spirit of the project to schoolchildren around the world. Under David's guidance, the educational programs associated with the flights proved very successful at stimulating the pioneers of tomorrow.

STEVE FOSSETT was a 12-year-old Boy Scout when he climbed his first mountain. For the next half century, he never stopped looking for new challenges. When Steve was in his teens, he discovered that he excelled at endurance activities and that he could achieve truly ambitious goals through planning, training, and sheer tenacity. Success on Chicago's trading exchanges (occasionally supported by driving a Yellow Cab) eventually allowed Steve to embark on a second career as a record-setting adventurer—"doing interesting things," as he liked to put it. In the way that some people collect art, he acquired endurance adventures, among them climbing Vinson Massif in Antarctica, swimming the English Channel, and completing the Iditarod Trail Sled Dog Race and Le Mans 24 Hours sports car race.

By the early 1990s, Steve began to focus less on races and checking goals off his private list, and instead set out to achieve significant world records or, even better, world firsts in sailing and flying. The result was more than two dozen major world records in sailing (including the absolute transatlantic and round-the-world marks), numerous speed and distance records, and the first ocean and continent crossings by balloon. He also held 11 world records in gliding (including the absolute glider altitude record at 50,727 feet), and transcontinental and global speed and distance records in powered aircraft, even an FAI-certified Zeppelin speed record of 71.5 miles per hour. Altogether, Steve held 116 major records and firsts.

Topping the list are the extraordinary first solo round-the-world balloon flight (Bud Light Spirit of Freedom, 2002, on his sixth attempt) and the first solo, nonstop, non-refueled, round-the-world airplane flight (Virgin Atlantic Global Flyer, 2005). Steve was a superb partner and pilot for the Vimy Atlantic project, which proved to be the ultimate test of skill, concentration, and endurance as he guided the machine for hour after hour through the darkness and clouds above the unforgiving ocean.

Steve Fossett died in a light aircraft on September 3, 2007. He is missed.

JOHN OWEN grew up in England reading "Biggles" volumes and tales of the Battle of Britain. After school, he took up a career in book publishing, which led him to a number of locations and ultimately to settle in Hong Kong for 20 years. John took the leap to establish his own company with Australian partner Kevin Weldon in 1985. Weldon Owen Publishing was launched in San Francisco, and in 1989 John met Peter McMillan for the first time. The two shared interests in aviation and high adventure, and when Lang and Peter first conceived of the Vimy project, John happened to be only a few miles away in Australia. He quickly endorsed this outrageous concept, but quickly added a dose of reality and business sense—after all, John had already undertaken such monumental projects as photographing the interior of mainland China from balloons in the early 1980s and producing the finest aerial picture book of Europe. John's experience was essential to the Vimy expeditions. He understood the surprisingly opaque goals of corporate sponsors, he knew the worlds of public relations and publishing, and he had previously developed a highly trusted relationship with *National Geographic*. Even more critical was his temperament: he was able to toggle the group back to reality and financial discipline when needed, or espouse the "amazing possibilities" when gloom or doubts crept into the room.

John earned hard-won success in business, but he remains as imaginative and nonlinear as any of the Vimy group. He has a habit of collecting beautiful, eclectic objects, such as functioning antique miniature steam trains that were typical gifts to Indian maharajas from viceroys seeking favors or a mid-18th-century, fully stocked carpenter's handmade tool chest, the man's last task as an apprentice. Best of all is John's 1941 de Havilland Tiger Moth, which he flies above the Hunter Valley in Australia.

JENNY MOSELEY is an idea person with the rare ability to turn outrageous ideas into actionable plans and to inspire others to work toward success. A bit of an aviation adventurer at heart, she worked closely with her colleagues at *National Geographic* during her 25-year career there to help make record-setting expeditions

such as transocean balloon attempts a success. She set up tracking stations to monitor the progress of world-famous balloonists Ed Yost, Joe Kittinger, Richard Branson, and the late Steve Fossett.

When Jenny was assigned by Mary Smith, who headed *National Geographic*'s expeditions division, and editor Bill Graves to be part of the NGS team on the first Vimy trip from England to Australia, she jumped at the chance, not realizing that she would later be intimately involved with the second trip from England to South Africa and the final leg across the Atlantic to Ireland. It turned out to be a 15-year adventure. Along the way, she was present at two takeoffs and three landings of the replica Vimy, an honor surpassed only by Mark Rebholz.

Jenny raised sponsorship funds for the Vimy; wrote, photographed, and edited; gave countless press and TV interviews and lectures; and planned logistics and support. She nurtured the young people who followed the South African flight; they called her the Silver Queen Mum. She inspired hundreds of volunteers to give their time and money in support of the Vimy's epic flights—and to project the spirit of adventure to the next generation of pioneers. Jenny runs a successful data and marketing consultancy in London until, perhaps, the next adventure comes along.

THE VIMY AIRCRAFT was described reverently by Captain Sir Ross Smith as "the nearest thing to animate life that man has created." It almost seems comical when one looks at this gigantic structure of wood and wires that he further called the Vimy "the zenith of man's constructional genius." Only 50 years later, "ordinary" men would travel on the Concorde at twice the speed of sound, and extraordinary men would land on the moon!

To the pilots who flew our faithful Vimy replica, she offered many special things—a chance to sharpen "real" airmanship while controlling a cumbersome, heavy, and slightly wandering flying machine. She also allowed the fliers the privilege of "borrowing" a seat from the pioneers and heroes who forever changed the way we move around the world—to feel what they felt, alone with the elements in a sense; to ride a time machine; and, perhaps best of all, to have a good, long look at the world, village by village, mountain by mountain, river by river, as if the earth were a great map being unrolled before the aircraft.

To those who saw the Vimy, she certainly engendered some curiosity: "You flew that from where?" But most people seemed to be intrigued on another level and quickly felt the sense of adventure and optimism, key elements to getting any new idea off the ground. Particularly fascinated were the youngsters, perhaps since the Vimy has no connection to their conception of an aircraft. It was as if something prehistoric had come to life. Children tended to linger with question after question. The twinkle from more than a few was a good indication that these kids wished to have adventures of their own in time.

A SPECIAL THANK-YOU

Design/Engineering/Construction Team

Clive Abraham
Jim Allen
John Anstam
Mark Arnold
Duncan Audette
Ted Baker
Chris Barnes
Bill Boitano
Charles Brakespeare
Ken Brown
Christian Bull
Ed Bullian
Daryl Christie
Ross Collin
Mark Compton
Ken Copp
Heinz Dachsel
Dot Daley
Ron Debruin
Jason Derry
Dr. Peter Dueker
Robert Dunlop
Erik Durfey
J. D. Durst
Brian and Beverley Esler
Malcolm Faiers
D. Kendall Farley
Adolf Fischer
Dick Fischer
John Ford
Billy Freeman
Paul Goyetche
Doug Griffin
Wolfgang Hall
Greg Hartwell
Dr. Christoph Hoerster
Bob and Madeleine
    Hopkins
Mike Jarvis
Jay Jerde
Bev Kidby
Jane Lucas
Ray Mandoux
Don McMakin
Dr. Thomas McMillan
Tom and Linda McMillan
Shawn Mulligan
Dan Nelson Jr.
Peter Norton
Ken Olson
Nick Olson
Del Ott

Dave Prinz
John Quinlisk
Chris Rehage
Brian Sanders
Dennis Sanders
Dick Sweetapple
Matthew Tomson
Bill Totton
Michael Urbschat
Richard Vickery
Kylee Waite
Carol and Bob Wallerman
Patrick Watson
Peter Watts
Korey Wells
Ed Whyschmeyer

Companies that Assisted Construction

AJD Engineering
Allied Signal/Bendix-King/
    AWA Inc.
The Australian Army
    Aviation Corps
Aviation Methods Inc.
Bay Avionics
BMW AG
British Airways
Bruntons (Musselburgh)
    Ltd.
Federal Express
J&E Hofmann
MT Propellers
Orenda Recip Engines
Perrone Leathers
Precision Fabrication
Retro Track and Air
Sheffield Engineering
Sigtronics Corporation
United Airlines

Individuals Who Assisted the Vimy Project

Riham el Aasar
Aidi Abdullah
His Excellency Hamad
    Rasheu Abu Nayyan
Giovanni Achibano
Dizzy Addicott
Jean-Luc Aeby
Patrick Albrand
Gregori Alegi
Huider Ali
Mirza Abdul Rasool Al Ali
Bill Allen

Ali Alqahtani
Tony Amos
Michael Anthimos
Majeed Abdulaziz
    Al Aqeel
Kim Arthur
Dr. Austin Asche
His Excellency Salim bin
    Ali Nasser Assiyabi
Lawrie Austin
His Excellency Joop Ave
Alan Aylieff
Francois Babel
George Bacon
Bob Bailey
Herman Bailey
Kim Bailie
Mike Balog
Mike Barber
Morag Barton
Mr. and Mrs. G. Batten
Mohammed Ali Al Belehi
David Bell
Group Captain John Bell
Garry Beverley
Atul Bindal
Gianni Bisogni
Richard Blacker
John Blake
Laura Boast
Judith Bobbitt
Richard and Tara Bonham
Captain Bonita
Spud Borer
Michael Boutin
Peter Boxer
Walter J. Boyne
Mary Brand
David Branigan
Mike Brannigan
Margaret Bridgman
Leslie Britton
Martin Brodie
George Brown
John Bull
Sue Burdekin
Seamus Burke
Robyne Burridge
Abdul Rahman Al Busaidy
Paul Cabot
Dave Calderwood
Eric Callaway
Billy Campbell
Group Captain Graeme
    Carroll

Peter Carter
Christopher Phua Chai
Sigrid Chase
Rajesh Chaturvedi
Chew Choong Cheng
John Chisolm
Twan Chu
Harold Clarke
Carroll Clifford
Rob Clot
Ian Coghill
Guy Cole
Peter Cole
Ross Collin
Aine Conroy
Joanne Coombs
Paul Cope
Mike Cottee
Group Captain
    Mac Cottrell
Helene Cox
Andrew Cranston
Leonard Curtis
Samara Daniel
Captain Russell Dann
Janet Davidson
Rick Davies
Rosemary Dawson
Ratan Dayal
Squadron Leader
    Kamal Deep
Jamie Denman
Steve Deveraux
Malcolm Dewhurst
Joe Dible
Tony Ditheridge
Ray Dolby
Ian Donabie
Mubarek N. Al Dossary
Superintendent
    Tony Dowd
Dan Downs
Surbita D'Souze
Marc Ducharme
Bill Duff
Glenda Duncan
Ken Durwood
Bob Dyer
Jim Eames
Brigadier Rod Earle
Shawn Elliott
Malcolm Ellis
Alyson Evans
Chris Evans

Iain Everingham
Michael Farlam
Bob Fassold
Mohamad Fazi
Greg Ferguson
Martin Fiddler
Richie Flaherty
Jim Flynn
Frank Foge
Mr. and Mrs. J. Foley
Fong Cheng Kee
Robert French
Steve Frennette
Dominic Fry
Mr. and Mrs. Duncan Fysh
Captain Abdul Rehman
    Al Gaoud
Kyle Gardner
Mark Garland
Simon Gaul
Jim Gavin
Ahmed Al Ghani
Captain Giovanni Giorgi
Bob Glindeman
Keith Gordon
Janet Green
Anne Greensall
Jodie Greer
Geoff Gregg
John Greissing
Darren Gribble
Keith Griggs
Stephane Guyon
Abdullah Saleh Al Hagiri
Wendy Hall
James Halley
Ibrahim Al Hamar
Linda Hannan
Bambang Harayadi
Tony Harkin
Bern Harmond
Keith Harris
Ron and Neville Harvey
Major Nagi Al Hashel
John Hasted
David Hebbard
Ron Hedges
Brian and Michele Hehir
Ray Heineger
Anne Hendrie
Major Brian Hicks
Dr. Hidayatullah
Thomas V. Higgins
Lil Hill

Patty Hill
Captain Victor Hines
Melvyn Hiscock
Captain Dick Hodder
Peter Holbrook
Andrew Holleyoak
Bernard Hougouneng
Max House
Franklin Huddle
Brian and Paul Hughes
Ian Hughes
Sally Hughes
Ambassador S.H.R. Hume
Hilary Hurt
Amanda Hutchinson
Anthony Hutton
Mrs. Charles Huxtable,
    O.A.M.
Moorooka Hyundai
Christopher Ian
Larry Ikels
Bob Ingle
Clive Jacques
Colonel Janacek
Dennis Johnson
Severin Johnson
Eleanor Jones
Sergeant Harri Keinonen
R. J. Kennette
Lance Kessler
Ian Kew
Shaikh Hamad bin
    Ebrahim Al Khalifa
Shaikh Mohammed bin
    Khalifa Al Khalifa
Shaikh Hamad bin
    Mohamed Al Khalifa
Fafar Khan
Katrina Kidby
Kylie Kidby
Gerald King
Peter Scott King
Jacquie Kirker
Robert and Shirley Kirker
Letda Kornelis
Ponlend Kositwongsakul
Peter Kroeff
Satish Kumar
Ambassador David
    Lamberston
Andy Lambert
Sergeant Cathy Landroche
Maria Langer
Brenda Anderson LaNoue

Commander LaSala
Garland and Molly Lasater
Alexis Laskaris
David Law
Ray Ledabrand
Rex LeDren
Lee Buck Choon
Tony Lee
George Legakis
Stan Letchford
O. T. Levent
Barry Levin
Jack Levin
Simon Littler
Debbie Liu
Audie Lloyd
Sir Richard Lloyd
Roni Lord
Melvyn Louis
Dawn Low
Peter Lowden
Christina Lucas
David, Joanna, Kate,
    Emma, Jim, and
    Nick Lumsden
Ken Lydall
Robin MacKay
Sir Christopher MacRael
Sean Maffett
Peter Magarrey
Pat Mannion
Mark Marshall
John Martin
Sir Peter Masefield
Fathi Mattar
Val Mattingly
Stephen Maycock
General Domenico Mazza
John and Laurie McBride
Ambassador
    C. E. McDonald
Ellen McDonough
Andrew McEachern
Terry McGlinn
Dick McGreal
Dave McKay
Karen McKenna
Dennis McNulty
Norris McWhirter
Gary Meermans
Vikram Mehta
Brigadier Kerry Mellor
Wendy Miles
John Mills

C. L. Moncrieff
Wayne Morris
Ian Mosely
A. Mouslidas
Shawn Mulligan
Donald Munro
Julie Munro
Muhamed Murad
Ken Murphy
Carmel Murray
David Nicholas
Lt. Colonel Dan Nichols
Lt. Colonel Dan Nichols
Larry Nighswander
Ambassador Thomas Niles
Michael Oakey
Jim Obata
P. R. S. Oberoi
Donal O'Connor
Rory O'Connor
Minister Eamonn O'Cuiv
Aidan and Maura
    O'Halloran
Mike O'Leary
Novotel Orchid
Ben Ostlind
Del Ott
Jeff Owen
John Owen
Jeremy Palmer
Frank Pangello
Captain Guiseppe Panico
Vic Parkes
John Patten
Norman Pealing
Frank Penny
Adrian Perez
Leroy Peterson
Connie Phelps
Joan Philip
Richard Phillips
Ambassador Mark Pierce
Norman Pointing
Dixie Porter
Erin Porter
Paul Porter
C. K. Poultney
Robert Pounds
John Powell
HM Idris Prawarto
Michael Prendergast
Daniel Prokop
Paddy Pryce
John Pulford
Jalal Qambar

Ali Abdulaziz Al Qasim
Rick Radell
Adriani Ramelan
Wing Commander
    S.S. Ramerao
Lorne Rastosky
Ken and Cynthia Rattey
Ms. E. Rawnsley
Colonel Renn
Garth Rhodes
David Richards
Judy and Roy Riddel
Ray Rimmell
Mohammed Ali Al Riyami
Jamie Roberts
Tim Roberts
George Robertson
Andrew Robson
Ron Rounds
Doc Rusted
David Ryan
Chrys Ryland
Jane Saberwahl
Abdul Khaliq Saeed
Mohamed Ali Salem
John Sandford
HRH Prince Mogrin bin
    Abdulaziz Al Saud
Captain P. Schlossbermel
Wayne Schumacher
Ken Schwartz
Ron Scobling
Catherine Sellman
Jules Senior
Brian Shadler
Abdul Kerim Khatim
    Al Shammery
Beverley Sharpe
Rod Sharpe
Nelson Sherren
His Excellency Yousuf
    Ahmed Al Shirawi
Tom Shone
Colonel Peter Simpson
Graham and Judy Sinclair
John Skeen
Adam Smith
Ken Snell
First Administrator
    Soedarko
Linda Sommerville
Mike Spick
Andrew Stevenson
Mike Stock

Paul Strickland
U. Suganda
Dr. Graeme Sweeney
Paul Swift
Bill Sykes and family
Warwick Tainton
Marion Tappin
Kitty Tawakley
Captain J. R. Taylor
Julian Temple
Teoh Eng Hongl
U. Thaung
Bob Thorne
U. Thura Aung Htet
Bill Tillotson
Phillipe Trelliet
Kevin Treloar
Craig Trickett
Mark Trumble
Otto and Yvonne Tschudi
David Tyler
John Ugi
Paul Ulrick
Mark Urban
Robert Urban
Richard van Oosterhout
Linda van Ryneveld
Tony van Ryneveld
Andrew Vickers
Richard Vickery
Heno Wahyuna
Lane Wallace
John Ware
Chris Warner
I. Warsa
Ambassador Warwick
    Weemaes
Kevin Weldon
Peter Westacott
Martin Whale
Caroline White
Jim Whittaker
Dr. Hariyo Wibowo
John Wilkinson
Mark Wilkinson
Peter Wilkinson
Angela Williams
Chuck Williams
Dean Williams
George Williams
Ted Williams
Allan Winn
Ted Wixted

Tessa Wood
Michael Woodhouse
    and family
Norm Worth
Roland Yap
Tina Ziolkowski

Corporate Sponsors
Aeroplane magazine
AIG Aviation
Air BP
The Bahrain Committee
BAIG
Bailey & Partners
Bose Aviation
Brooklands Museum
Gieves & Hawkes
Gulf Air
National Geographic
    Society
Police Aviation Services
Qantas
Rolls-Royce Group plc
Royal Mail
SBAC
Shell International
TAG Aviation
USAIG
U.S. Air Force
Weldon Owen Publishing

Museums, Clubs, Agencies, and Corporations That Supported the Vimy Project
Aero Club of East Africa,
    Kenya
Aero Club di Roma
Aeronautical Society of
    Calcutta
BBC Radio
British Aerospace
Bulawayo Club, Zimbabwe
Caboolture Aero Club
Cairo Glider Club
Clifden Fire Brigade
Coffs Harbour City
CRS Ltd
Driza-Bone
The Explorer's Club
First Aviation Regiment,
    Oakey, Queensland
French Air Force, Djibouti
Great War Flying
    Machines

Groupe Accor
Kenyan Wildlife Services
La Ferté-Alais Airfield,
    France
The Lima Zulu Appeal
London Berrima Aero Club
Longreach Shire Council
Mena House Oberoi
Missionary Aviation
    Fellowship
Museum of Army Flying
Museum of Science and
    Industry, London
Narrandera Shire Council
Narromine Aero Club
Nile Valley Aviation
Oberschliessheim
    Museum, Munich
Parkes Aero Club National
    Rescue
Pol Roger Champagne
Royal Air Force Museum
Royal Geographic Society
Royal Newcastle Aero
    Club
Royal Queensland Aero
    Club
Save the Elephants
The William E. Simon
    and Carol G. Simon
    Foundation
Singapore Flying Club
Smithsonian National Air
    and Space Museum
Snap-on Tools
Sotheby's
South African Air Force
Stellenbosch Flying Club
Thameshead Inn, Kemble,
    England
Trafalgar House
Tropic Air, Kenya
29th Air Wing, Allahabad,
    India
United Nations
U.S. Embassy in Djibouti
Vickers Plc
Victoria Falls Helis
World Wildlife Fund

Scores of people contibuted to the success of the Vimy project, including those who inadvertently have been omitted here.

INDEX

AVIATION ADVENTURES

Conceived, produced, and published by
Aviation Adventures LLC
120 Bulkley Avenue #405
Sausalito, CA 94965, USA
415.331.3883
www.vimy.org

Copyright © 2011 Aviation Adventures LLC

Editor Judith Dunham

Art Director Kari Ontko, Ontko Design

Picture Researchers Joanna Collard, Philip Jarrett, Ashley Parada

Production Consultants Teri Bell, Chris Hemesath

Production Assistant Joan Olson

Proofreader Linda Bouchard

Indexer Ken DellaPenta

Maps David Atkinson

Authors Mick Follari, Philip Jarrett, John LaNoue, Peter McBride, Peter McMillan, Mark Rebholz

Publisher John Owen

Sales & Marketing Dawn Owen

Advisor David Holbrooke MD

For information about special discounts for bulk purchases, please contact Special Sales at Aviation Adventures LLC, www.vimy.org or 415.331.3883.

All rights reserved. No part of this publication may be reproduced or transmitted in any form or by any means, electronic or mechanical, including photocopying, or by any information storage or retrieval system, without permission in writing from the copyright holder.

First printed in 2011

Color reproduction by Mission Productions Ltd, Hong Kong
Printed in China by 1010 Printing Limited

Library of Congress Cataloging-in-publication data available

ISBN: 978-0-9832362-0-7

AUTHOR'S NOTE

The flights of the Vimy and this book would not have been possible without the National Geographic Society and the enterprise and skill of the staff members who helped us preserve such vivid records of the adventures. We were supported across many divisions of National Geographic, and we would like to recognize in particular the efforts of Gil Grosvenor, Bill Graves, Tim Kelly, Bill Allen, Mary Smith, Jim Stanfield, Chris Weber, Bob Poole, Joe Stancampiano, Connie Phelps, Jenny Moseley, Ashley Parada, and Barbara Moffet.

I would like to thank Brian Cocks, Sheena Coupe, Martin Farley of Denzil Print Ltd, Alan Farnham, Tim Hall, Lang Kidby, Michael Oakey and Amanda Lock of *Aeroplane Monthly*, Lurlyn Reyes, and Kevin Weldon for their generous help in producing this book. I also express my appreciation to the authors, photographers, and other contributors from around the world who helped bring this book to fruition, to serve as a lasting memory of these expeditions and to inspire dreams and adventures for the future. —Peter McMillan

PHOTO AND ILLUSTRATION CREDITS

The photographs and illustrations are courtesy of (t: top, b: bottom, c: center, l: left, r: right)

Sebastien Arsenault 170b, 216tl, 217b, 218, 219tr, 220; **David Branigan, Oceansport** 6, 200, 201r, 201cl, 204r, 206, 202; **Alan Brown** 98t, 98b; **Eric Coeckelberghs** 246t, 246b, 247tl, 247r, 247cl; **Eric Dumigan** 175c, 176, 179tl, 179bl, 180, 181tl, 181tc, 181tr, 181br, 181bl; **Eric Durfey** 16, 23t, 26, 86, 87tl, 87cr, 87br, 87bl, 87cl, 88, 90tl, 90tr, 90br, 90bl, 91l, 91r, 94l, 94tr, 94cr, 94br, 95, 213row3, 213row4, 243tc, 243tr, 243cl, 243c, 243cr, 243bl, 243bc, 243br; **Flitzer** 216cl, 217r, 217cl, 217c; **Mick Follari** 20, 114, 116bl, 132bl, 150bl, 154row1l, 154row1r, 154row2c, 154row2r, 154row3l, 154row3r, 154row4c, 155row1l, 155row1r, 155row2l, 155row2r, 155row3l, 155row4l, 155row4r, 157tr, 157br, 162, 164t, 164br, 164bl, 211tl, 213row1r, 213row2l; **Paul Garner** 174tl, 174cl, 216tr; **Martin Goebel** 174bl, 174r; **David Hebbard** 175t, 175b, 188, 190, 195, 249l; **Myron Heimer** 171tl, 171tr; **Philip Jarrett** 103l, 103tr, 103br, 104tl, 104bl, 104r, 104t, 104b, 184, 185tl, 185cr, 185b, 185cl, 186t, 186b, 187t, 187b, 222, 224tl, 224cl, 224bl, 224r, 225tl, 225tr, 225b, 225cl, 226tl, 226tr, 226c, 226br, 226bl, 227t, 227c, 227b, 228t, 228b, 229tl, 229tr, 229b, 230l, 230tr, 230cr, 230br, 231t, 231c, 231b; **Jim Koepnick** 99, 166, 167t, 167b, 171br, 182, 196, 198; **John LaNoue** 170tl, 170tc, 170tr, 214tl, 214tr, 214br, 214bl, 215, 216br, 219br, 236br, 238br, 239l, 239tr, 242br, 243tl; **Peter McBride** 12, 24, 100, 108, 110, 112, 113tl, 113tr, 113br, 113bl, 116t, 116br, 117tl, 117tc, 117tr, 117b, 118, 119, 120, 121tl, 121tr, 121b, 122t, 122br, 122bl, 123, 124, 125tl, 125tr, 125br, 125bl, 126t, 126cr, 126br, 126bl, 127, 128, 129t, 129c, 129b, 130tl, 130tr, 130br, 130bc, 130bl, 131, 132t, 132br, 132bc, 133, 134l, 134r, 135t, 135c, 135b, 136l, 136r, 137, 138, 140tl, 140tr, 140br, 140bl, 141, 142tl, 142tr, 142br, 142bl, 143, 144, 146t, 146b, 147, 148tl, 148r, 148bl, 149t, 149b, 150tl, 150tr, 150br

151t, 151b, 152, 153, 154row1c, 154row2l, 154row3c, 154row4l, 154row4r, 155row3r, 156, 157tl, 157bl, 158, 165tl, 165r, 165bl, 171bl, 194, 211tc, 213row1l; **Peter McMillan** 29tr, 211bc, 216cr, 216bl; **Mitchell Library, State Library of New South Wales** 33b; **Jenny Moseley** 249br; **Frank Munger, Flightline Arts** 232–33; **National Geographic Society** 1, 2, 4, 8 & 70, 10, 18, 22l & 236l, 22tr, 22cr, 22br, 28, 29tl, 29tc, 29b, 30b, 31tl, 31tr, 31br, 31bl, 32l, 32tc, 32tr, 32b, 33t, 36, 37t, 37b, 38, 40, 42, 43, 44, 45t, 45br, 45bl, 46, 48, 49tl, 49tr, 49br, 49bl, 50, 51, 52, 53t, 53b, 54t, 54c, 54b, 55, 56, 57l, 57t, 57br, 58tl, 58l, 58tr, 58cr, 58br, 59t, 59b, 60, 62, 63t, 63bl, 63bc, 63bc, 63br, 64, 65t, 65b, 66, 67, 68, 69t, 69b, 71t, 71b, 72t, 72br, 72bl, 73tl, 73tr, 73cr, 73br, 73bl, 74tl, 74tr, 74br, 74bc, 75t, 75br, 75bc, 75bl, 76, 77, 78, 79t, 79cr, 79br, 79bl, 80, 82, 83tl, 83tr, 83cr, 83bl, 83cl, 84, 87tr, 92, 96, 208, 210, 211tr, 211bl, 212t, 212b, 223, 234, 236tr, 237tl, 237r, 237bl, 238l, 238tr, 239br, 240, 242t, 242bl, 245; **Paul Nicol** 192; **George Norman** 201tl, 201bl, 204tl, 204cl, 204bl, 205bl; **Michael Oakey** 14, 199, 205t, 205br, 247bc, 247bl; **John Owen** 213row2r, 249tr; **Francois Prins** 219l; **Rick Radell** 178, 179r; **Tom Saunders, Canada Aviation Museum** 172t; **Science & Society Picture Library/Getty Images** 185tr; **State Library of South Australia** 30t, 256; **Ken Swartz** 217tl; **Gary M. Tahir, Altitude Graphics** 160, 172br, 72bl; **Topical Press Agency/Hulton Archive/Getty Images** 102; **Jim Turner** 23b, 168, 169tl, 169tr, 169b, 173.

Aviation Adventures has made every effort to correctly identify and credit the sources of the photographs used in this book. Any errors should be brought to the attention of the publisher.